Jesus Speaking

Heart to Heart
with the King

From the Writings of Gabrielle Bossis
Edited by Maria Grace Dateno, FSP

Pauline
BOOKS & MEDIA

Boston

Library of Congress Cataloging-in-Publication Data

Names: Bossis, Gabrielle, 1874-1950, author. | Dateno, Maria Grace, editor.
Title: Jesus speaking : heart to heart with the King / written by Gabrielle Bossis ;
edited by Maria Grace Dateno, FSP. Other titles: Lui et moi. Selections. English.
Description: Boston : Pauline Books & Media, [2019] | "Excerpts are taken from He and I
by Gabrielle Bossis published by Pauline Books & Media which was originally published as
Lui et Moi by Beauchesne et ses Fils."
Identifiers: LCCN 2019006145 | ISBN 9780819840318 (pbk.) | ISBN 0819840319 (pbk.)
Subjects: LCSH: Devotional calendars. | Jesus Christ--Meditations.
Classification: LCC BV4811 .B62313 2019 | DDC 242/.2--dc23

LC record available at https://lccn.loc.gov/2019006145

Excerpts are taken from *He and I* by Gabrielle Bossis (© Éditions Médiaspaul, 250, rue.
Saint-François Nord, Sherbrooke, QC, J1E 2B9 [Canada]). Reprinted by Pauline Books &
Media. *He and I* is a condensed version of the original French edition *Lui et Moi* published by
Beauchesne et ses Fils, 117 rue de Rennes, Paris.

Cover design and art by Danielle Victoria Lussier, FSP

Handlettering by Marie Heimann of Fawnly Prints

Published by Pauline Books & Media, 50 Saint Pauls Avenue, Boston, MA 02130-3491

Printed in the U.S.A.

www.pauline.org

Pauline Books & Media is the publishing house of the Daughters of St. Paul, an international
congregation of women religious serving the Church with the communications media.

1 2 3 4 5 6 7 8 9   23 22 21 20 19

Contents

Foreword

I'm a lover of books, and books have changed the course of my life on more than one occasion. Some books I read once and pass on. Other books I just can't let go of.

He and I, the classic work by Gabrielle Bossis that is the basis for this devotional, definitely falls into that second category. I came across a copy of *He and I* during my first year in the convent, and forty-five years later it is still one of the most beloved titles on my book shelf!

Although *He and I* is a conversation between Gabrielle and Jesus, as the reader I can't help but feel that Jesus is talking directly to me in a personal, intimate way. Heart to heart. Friend to friend. Lover to lover. It's something I don't think we ever outgrow:

this need of our heart to hear the voice of the One we love.

People are so hungry for a real, vibrant relationship with the Lord but can be at a loss as to how to go about it. How do you pray when you feel tired and distracted? What do you read to quiet your heart and focus on Jesus? And how do you even start a conversation with Him with all the worries and problems that clamor for your attention even before your morning coffee?

I've spent many years working in our Pauline Books & Media centers across the United States, and I've heard countless requests for a book that could help people who

— have lost their spouses,

— just discovered they have cancer,

— have lost hope in life,

— would like to pray but don't know where to start,

— want a devotional that will get them through the day,

— have been disappointed,

— need something inspiring to give as a gift,

— need a prayer-starter for Eucharistic Adoration,

— want a book for someone who doesn't like to read (this one always has me shaking my head).

Well, I can honestly say, THIS book fits the bill for all the above!

Each one of us is special to Jesus. He wants a personal, close relationship with you and with me. The short daily text in *Jesus Speaking* is meant to be savored and carried in your heart. It is a collection of word gems that will open your heart to feeling loved and cherished by the Lord. And everyone longs for that because we were all made for Him.

JULIA MARY DARRENKAMP, FSP

Preface

Gabrielle Bossis was born in France in 1874, into a fairly well-to-do family. She remained single all her life and had many interests and pursuits, such as the fine arts of painting and music, horseback riding, and embroidery. She was very active in her parish and socially. During World War I, she worked as a nurse.

Later in life Gabrielle began writing, producing, and acting in plays. She traveled internationally for her work, and her plays were much in demand. During this time, her many friends and acquaintances were completely unaware of a very deep interior life that was beneath all these activities. She had always been inclined to prayer and contemplation, but beginning in her early sixties, Gabrielle frequently heard Jesus speaking to her, and she wrote down the words she understood Him to say—a practice she continued until her death in 1950.

Gabrielle knew these words were intended not just for herself, but for everyone, so she anonymously published a collection of the messages toward the end of her life. It was called *Lui et Moi* and was very well-received. After her death, more volumes came out and were translated and distributed widely.

In English, the one-volume edition that is condensed from the several French volumes is called *He and I* and has become a modern classic. Even today, many people who read the words that Jesus spoke to Gabrielle feel as if these words are personally addressed to them.

Jesus Speaking is an effort to introduce new readers to these loving words by providing short selections from *He and I*, together with Scripture passages, for each day of the year. The index in the back of this book indicates where each *He and I* selection is taken from. The messages in *He and I* are dated according to when Gabrielle wrote them.

How to Use This Book

Below are some suggestions for using this book for daily prayer. Feel free to follow anything helpful and leave aside anything that is not.

— If you do not already have one, it's good to decide on a set time for daily prayer—at the same time each day, if possible. The time you spend with Jesus is vital to your spiritual life, so it's better to schedule time for it and sometimes have to delay or skip it, rather than just "try to fit it in" between the tasks of the day. It doesn't have to be a long period of time—start with ten minutes if that is what is possible for you. Early morning before your day gets going is a good time. Another possibility is before you go to bed.

— When you sit down to pray, take a moment to prepare by breathing deeply a few times and calling to mind that you are in God's presence. Jesus has been looking forward to this moment. Take any concerns or tasks or annoyances that are in your thoughts and imagine placing them in His hands. You can let go of them for now and take them back later (if you want to!).

— Read the Scripture passage and then the selection from *He and I*. Read slowly, out loud, if feasible. Read them over a few times.

— If a word or phrase strikes you, pause and stay with it for a while.

— Notice what stirs in your heart. It could be joy, consolation, anger, surprise, confusion, hope, disappointment, desire, love, frustration . . . anything! Whatever is in your mind and heart, show it to Jesus. Ask Him about it, talk to Him about it, or just sit with Him in the midst of it. Pay attention to anything Jesus says to you or points out to you.

— If nothing in particular strikes you in the reading, or if you need something to help you enter into the passage, read the prayer prompt at the bottom and then read the Scripture and the quotation again. If you don't notice or feel any particular stirring, just tell Jesus you are happy to sit with Him quietly. If you have difficulty escaping from your distracting thoughts and concerns, just keep putting them back in Jesus' hands and tell Him you are happy just to be able to be with Him.

— Toward the end of your prayer time, you might consider writing in a journal something about what moved you and what you felt Jesus was saying to you. You could also write any decisions or resolutions you have made, regarding how you want to respond to these gifts in the day ahead. For example, your response could be an action or an interior change of attitude.

— At the end, thank Jesus for the time spent with Him, and pray:

Glory be to the Father, and to the Son, and to the Holy Spirit: as it was in the beginning, is now, and ever shall be, world without end. Amen.

Ask for Mary's intercession that the graces of your prayer may bear fruit. You can use this prayer or one of your favorite prayers to Our Lady:

> *Remember, O most gracious Virgin Mary,*
> *that never was it known*
> *that anyone who fled to thy protection,*
> * implored thy help,*
> *or sought thy intercession, was left unaided.*
> *Inspired by this confidence I fly unto thee,*
> *O Virgin of virgins, my Mother.*
> *To thee do I come, before thee I stand, sinful and*
> * sorrowful.*
> *O Mother of the Word Incarnate,*
> *despise not my petitions, but in thy mercy hear and*
> * answer me. Amen.*

JANUARY

January 1

"If you abide in me, and my words abide in you, ask for whatever you wish, and it will be done for you. My Father is glorified by this, that you bear much fruit and become my disciples. As the Father has loved me, so I have loved you; abide in my love" (Jn 15:7–9).

So great is My longing to have you come nearer. I have so much to say to you, so much to give you . . . Come. Nearer, always nearer . . .

Tell Jesus how close to Him you want to be, and then remain silent and listen.

January 2

And over all these put on love, that is, the bond of perfection (Col 3:14).

Do you realize that love is the one and only goal and that everything should serve to lead you to it? A very little thing becomes big if it takes you to love. And an important work is absolutely nothing if it fails to lead to love.

Look at the big and little things of the day ahead, and offer them to Him with love.

January 3

My heart is steadfast, O God, my heart is
        steadfast;
    I will sing and make melody.
    Awake, my soul! (Ps 108:1).

Your longing to love—this is love . . . In your soul
there is a door that leads to the contemplation of
God. But you must open it.

*When you realize that longing to love is love,
what stirs within you?*

January 4

The steadfast love of the LORD never ceases,
    his mercies never come to an end
      (Lam 3:22).

Love calls to love. Answer Me, child. I am thirsty for you. What intimidates you? Your repeated neglectfulness? Your deficiencies, your vagueness, your absentmindedness, your distressing memories? I take charge of everything. I collect miseries and make glorious things out of them.

Imagine what it would be like to have Jesus make "glorious things" out of the miseries in your life.

January 5

"If any want to become my followers, let them deny themselves and take up their cross daily and follow me" (Lk 9:23).

A sacrifice joyously made is no longer a sacrifice. It is only what one refuses that is costly—what one does halfheartedly. So up with your cross on your shoulder, and on your way! Near Me, always nearer to Me.

How can you respond to what Jesus is asking?
Ask Him for the help you need to do so.

January 6

The LORD is my strength and my shield;
    in him my heart trusts;
so I am helped, and my heart exults,
    and with my song I give thanks to him
    (Ps 28:7).

Give Me the joy of helping and transforming you. Surrender everything. Let yourself go. Tell Me often about your great longing. Do you think I would resist?

What would it be like to trust Jesus this much?

January 7

[H]e said to me, "My grace is sufficient for you, for power is made perfect in weakness" (2 Cor 12:9).

If you have failed in something, you say, "My dear all, I could have been more faithful today. Forgive me." You humble yourself most sincerely. And without your knowing it, I press you to My heart burning with love. That is what you call grace, and My grace is sufficient for you. Do you believe that?

Imagine Jesus pressing you to His heart. What would that be like?

January 8

"I give you a new commandment, that you love one another. Just as I have loved you, you also should love one another" (Jn 13:34).

Offer Me all the crosses of the world. There are so many just now and few think of offering them to Me in expiation for sins. You who do know, help, so that nothing may be lost. Give Me hearts. Give Me souls. I am thirsty. Always.

Call to mind the current sufferings and tragedies around the world, and offer all the affected people to Him.

January 9

So whether you eat or drink, or whatever you do, do everything for the glory of God (1 Cor 10:31).

Even by your ordinary actions you can make amends for ingratitude and save sinners. I saved while sweeping the workshop. Always be one with Me.

Tell Jesus how much you appreciate knowing the value of even your smallest actions.

January 10

When the LORD restored the fortunes of
    Zion,
  we were like those who dream.
Then our mouth was filled with laughter,
  and our tongue with shouts of joy;
then it was said among the nations,
    "The LORD has done great things for them"
    (Ps 126:1–2).

Tell Me why you love Me and how this love began;
tell Me all that you want to do for My love. Of
course, I know all about it, but to hear it from you
is a joy to Me, like a story ever new.

*Have you ever thought of your relationship
with Him as a story? Talk to Him about it.*

January 11

And Mary said,
"My soul magnifies the Lord,
    and my spirit rejoices in God my Savior,
for he has looked with favor on the lowliness
    of his servant (Lk 1:46–48).

Above all, don't ever grow weary of our intimacy. Vary. Improvise. Perfect. Increase. Call upon the Spirit of love to help you. Ask My mother to show you—she who never left Me. Even when you feel good for nothing, give Me this nothing. Didn't I create with nothing?

What is one thing in your relationship with Jesus that you could vary or increase?

January 12

"They who have my commandments and keep them are those who love me; and those who love me will be loved by my Father, and I will love them and reveal myself to them" (Jn 14:21).

Be one with Me in My toil as a carpenter. It is not what you do that matters, but the way you love Me while you work. And love is oneness.

Look at the day ahead, choose one task or duty, and decide how you can love while you work.

January 13

"Ask, and it will be given you; search, and you will find; knock, and the door will be opened for you. For everyone who asks receives, and everyone who searches finds, and for everyone who knocks, the door will be opened" (Mt 7:7–8).

W hy do you ask so little? Come to Us, My child, and ease Our longing to show compassion. Don't ever forget that the people around you are there in order that you may plead for them.

Be extravagant! What's the biggest thing you can ask from God? Ask for it right now.

January 14

So then, while we have the opportunity, let us do good to all, but especially to those who belong to the family of the faith (Gal 6:10).

And if you are the means of bringing one or many into frequent fellowship with Me, do you think that I could fail to be grateful, not only for the glory gained by it, but above all for the joy it brings to My heart.

Did you ever consider that you could bring Him joy this way?

January 15

The meek shall obtain fresh joy in the LORD,
and the neediest people shall exult in the
Holy One of Israel (Isa 29:19).

Fall in love with your God—this glorious Reality.
And if you are in love with Him, you will think
about Him more often. It is this remembrance of
Me that I want in you, this desire to please Me, this
fear that people offend Me, this joy in My
kingdom.

*What would it look like for you to fall in love
with God?*

January 16

The LORD went in front of them in a pillar of cloud by day, to lead them along the way, and in a pillar of fire by night, to give them light, so that they might travel by day and by night (Ex 13:21).

Let yourself be taken swiftly. Instead of running away, throw yourself into My arms and lose your bearings. I'll love you like that—blind, letting Me lead you.

Throw yourself into the arms of Jesus, handing over to Him all your concerns.

January 17

Humble yourselves before the Lord, and he will exalt you (Jas 4:10).

Humble yourself for your shortcomings. It is your faults, My children, that make you unhappy. . . . Look at your shortsightedness. Your cowardice and laziness in making any effort to improve. Your willingness to stagnate in your usual petty ways. Your negligence in studying the model of My life.

What makes you unhappy? With courage, show these things to Him.

January 18

For your steadfast love is as high as the
heavens;
your faithfulness extends to the clouds
(Ps 57:10).

Tell Me that at last you believe in My immense
love ever-present in you, that you are always sure of
it. My grace would increase in proportion, even to
the point of a miracle, for what is a miracle but a
token of love's simplicity?

How can you respond to what Jesus is saying?
Show Him what is in your heart.

January 19

"I in them and you in me, that they may become completely one, so that the world may know that you have sent me and have loved them even as you have loved me. Father, I desire that those also, whom you have given me, may be with me where I am" (Jn 17:23–24).

Why do you talk to Me as though I were so far away? I'm very near . . . in your heart. Don't feel sad about a distraction even if it lasts some time. Just pick up your loving contemplation where you left off.

Thank Jesus for His promise to be always in your heart.

January 20

Teach us to count our days
that we may gain a wise heart (Ps 90:12).

God . . . When you see Him, how you will want to have served Him, to have loved Him, to have glorified Him without counting the cost, and with all your heart! Don't be afraid of trials. They only help you to go higher. They make you love Me more.

What are you facing today, and how will you have wanted to act when you look back at the end of your life?

January 21

Have no anxiety at all, but in everything, by prayer and petition, with thanksgiving, make your requests known to God (Phil 4:6).

Don't get the idea that it is the greatest number of prayers that touches your God. It's the way you speak to Him. Be irresistible in love, abandonment, and humility.

What would being "irresistible in love, abandonment, and humility" look like for you?

January 22

"Let your light shine before others, so that they may see your good works and give glory to your Father in heaven" (Mt 5:16).

My child, don't lose a single minute. Time is short for saving so many souls. It is not merely by praying that they are saved, you know, but through the actions of even the most ordinary lives lived for God.

Ask for guidance in your prayers and actions today, to do all for God and the salvation of others.

January 23

May all who seek you
    rejoice and be glad in you;
may those who love your salvation
    say continually, "Great is the LORD!"
        (Ps 40:16).

Are you quite ready to understand that joys can serve Me as well as trials if you give them to Me, if you live them for Me? If you recognize them as My special gifts, and if you love Me more because of them?

Find five joys (even small ones) in your life right now that you can live for Jesus.

January 24

"I am the bread of life. Whoever comes to me will never be hungry, and whoever believes in me will never be thirsty" (Jn 6:35).

The thirst for union with you is so great that I want to be consumed by you in order to merge our minds, our beings. I want to be your thinking and your doing. Such love amazes you, and yet you can guess at only a very faint part of it.

Be amazed that you only know a very small part of His love. What more is there? Do you desire to know it?

January 25

If my people who are called by my name humble themselves, pray, seek my face, and turn from their wicked ways, then I will hear from heaven, and will forgive their sin and heal their land (2 Chr 7:14).

Ask Me for everything you have lost through neglecting to harmonize with My grace. Ask humbly, with confidence, and My compassionate heart will give it to you because with love nothing is impossible and My love is victorious.

What do you feel you have lost? Thank Him for His victorious love.

January 26

"No one has greater love than this, to lay down one's life for one's friends" (Jn 15:13).

I have so great a desire to give Myself. If you only knew the effort it was for Me—not to give to you, but to refrain from giving . . . That is why your requests relieve Me.

Call to Jesus now and let Him give Himself to you exactly as He wishes.

January 27

The disciples rejoiced when they saw the Lord
(Jn 20:20).

Look at the cycle of My life. What have you loved
the most? My humble birth, My hidden life, the
public revelation, or My shameful death? Wherever
you look, can you see any other hallmark than
love?... So be full of joy. Respond to the avalanche
of My gifts.

Ask Him to help you respond to the avalanche
of His gifts.

January 28

My soul longs, indeed it faints
    for the courts of the LORD;
my heart and my flesh sing for joy
    to the living God (Ps 84:2).

Enter into my courts. Ask the help of My mother. Go farther, still farther. Leave material things behind. Go right into the most secret shrine.

Do you have any hesitation in responding to His invitation? Ask Mary's help.

January 29

I will come praising the mighty deeds of
the Lord GOD,
   I will praise your righteousness, yours
alone.
O God, from my youth you have taught me,
   and I still proclaim your wondrous deeds
    (Ps 71:16–17).

You remember when you were little, you said to
Me: "Incline my heart, O Lord, to the words of
Your mouth." Listen and I'll speak to you. Would
you like to be My confidante?

*Thank Him for choosing you to be His
confidante.*

January 30

"Whenever you pray, go into your room and shut the door and pray to your Father who is in secret; and your Father who sees in secret will reward you" (Mt 6:6).

Begin by closing all the gates of the senses to the outer world. Then place Me before your soul like a sure presence. Finally, enter deeply into Me.

Close your eyes and ask Jesus to help you enter deeply into Him.

January 31

Jesus said to her, "I am the resurrection and the life. Those who believe in me, even though they die, will live, and everyone who lives and believes in me will never die" (Jn 11:25–26).

Don't be surprised at setbacks; you were made for rest in heaven not on earth. So get used to living for eternity; for nothing has the slightest importance in time that does not count for eternity. Judge everything in Me and by Me.

What difficulties are you facing right now? How will they look from the other side of eternity?

FEBRUARY

February 1

For the mountains may depart
    and the hills be removed,
but my steadfast love shall not depart
      from you,
    and my covenant of peace shall not be
      removed,
    says the LORD, who has compassion on you
      (Isa 54:10).

I'm nearer to you than you are, and every tender word My children say to Me delights and charms My heart. Don't ever doubt it.

What do you want to say to Him today? He is very near, listening.

February 2

Trust in the LORD forever,
  for in the LORD GOD
  you have an everlasting rock (Isa 26:4).

There I am, waiting for you at the bend in the road. "How will she overcome this difficulty? Will she ask Me to help her? Will she give Me her whole confidence at last in a childlike outburst of tenderness?" Oh, the serenity of the one who has yielded everything to Me.

Turn to Him with confidence about any difficulty you have in your life right now.

February 3

Trust in the LORD with all your heart,
and do not rely on your own insight.
In all your ways acknowledge him,
and he will make straight your paths
(Prov 3:5–6).

When something needs mending, one puts it into the hands of a craftsman. Put your soul, silent and still, beneath my loving look. I repair.

What would it be like to sit silently under His loving look? Try it right now.

February 4

"If you loved me, you would rejoice that I am going to the Father, because the Father is greater than I" (Jn 14:28).

Won't you honor Me in this new way, in this joy for My joy? And if there is joy in you, how can you stop it from brimming over on others? Do you think I find very much joy in many hearts? People don't think of this perfect way of praising Me and yet it brings Me such balm.

Ask God to increase your joy as a way of praising Him.

February 5

"Whatever you ask for in prayer, believe that you have received it, and it will be yours" (Mk 11:24).

You understand—in Me you can find everything: all the love you need to help you. So don't be afraid of making use of the one who loves you so. Unfold your trust like silk to clothe your request, and you will vanquish Me.

What is your deepest need right now? Make your request with great confidence.

February 6

The sun shall no longer be
    your light by day,
nor for brightness shall the moon
    give light to you by night;
but the LORD will be your everlasting light,
    and your God will be your glory
        (Isa 60:19).

Let us begin heaven. Moment by moment, love
Me while I'm loving you.

*Love Him right now, in this moment, and
let Him love you. Ask Him what you want to
know about heaven.*

February 7

In the same way, the Spirit too comes to the aid of our weakness; for we do not know how to pray as we ought, but the Spirit itself intercedes with inexpressible groanings (Rom 8:26).

So don't be reticent. If you want Me, tell Me so. I mean pray—sink deep down into the remembrance of Me and talk to Me in a direct look.

Do you feel hesitant to pray like this? Ask the Holy Spirit to teach you how.

February 8

"I am the bread of life" (Jn 6:48).

All night long I waited for you in My Eucharist—waited to give Myself to you in the morning. Why should this astonish you? You believe in My presence in the tabernacle, don't you? You believe in My immense love? Then put the two together. And when you wake up during the night, look at the one who is already longing for the dawn to bring you to Him.

Picture Jesus waiting for you. What do you want to say to Him?

February 9

One man was there who had been ill for thirty-eight years. When Jesus saw him lying there and knew that he had been there a long time, he said to him, "Do you want to be made well?" (Jn 5:5–6).

Although it may seem strange to you, there is grace that I cannot give unless you ask Me for it.

Are there graces you have assumed God would never grant you, or that He would give without your asking for them? Ask Him for them right now.

February 10

Let my prayer be counted as incense before
       you,
  and the lifting up of my hands as an
      evening sacrifice (Ps 141:2).

Don't say "Glory to the Father and to the Son" in such a vague way, but wish for this glory in this and that action of yours.

Resolve that all your actions this day will be done for His glory, not just in general, but each individual act of your day.

February 11

"From now on all generations will call me
blessed;
for the Mighty One has done great things
for me,
and holy is his name" (Lk 1:48–49).

Quicken the fire of your love with Mine. Ask for
everything through My mother. She is so good, so
attentive in caring for your souls. If only you knew!
You don't know her well enough. Give yourself to
her without reserve, like her little Jesus.

*Talk with Mary, the mother of Jesus, about
how you need her help and want to know her
better.*

February 12

Then he took a loaf of bread, and when he had given thanks, he broke it and gave it to them, saying, "This is my body, which is given for you. Do this in remembrance of me" (Lk 22:19).

Look how alone I am in this empty church. I knew it would be like this. And yet I instituted My Eucharist. I would feed even a single soul.

Kneel in spirit before the tabernacle in every empty church of the world.

February 13

Indeed, the grace of our Lord has been abundant, along with the faith and love that are in Christ Jesus. This saying is trustworthy and deserves full acceptance: Christ Jesus came into the world to save sinners. Of these I am the foremost (1 Tim 1:14–15).

I always forgive if you tell Me of your neglect and feel truly sorry for it. I'm not one of those who spy on faults and failings, ready to be severe. I am all goodness.

Do you imagine Jesus watching to see what you are doing wrong? Instead thank Him for His goodness and tenderness.

February 14

Set me as a seal upon your heart,
    as a seal upon your arm;
for love is strong as death,
    passion fierce as the grave.
Its flashes are flashes of fire,
    a raging flame (Song 8:6).

Don't ever grow weary of Me, My friend. Fall in love with Me over and over again, and let your way of loving Me always be new.

Are you feeling weary? Take some moments to remember and reflect on when you first loved Him.

February 15

From the rising of the sun to its setting
  the name of the LORD is to be praised
    (Ps 113:3).

Divide your day into three parts. In the morning, as soon as you awaken, give yourself to the Father Creator, who offers you His Son as food. After Mass, give yourself to the Son, who is in you. And fall asleep in the Holy Spirit, who is love.

How would your day be different if it was lived in this way?

February 16

"Just as the living Father sent me, and I live because of the Father, so whoever eats me will live because of me" (Jn 6:57).

Seek Me always in the Eucharist. It is there for you, for everyone. Don't be reticent. Come simply. Give thanks with joy in your heart. Love simply. Everything is so simple with Me. Don't you notice this when I speak to you? Leave behind your old way of imagining. Enter into the way of love's clear vision.

Go to Him and simply listen. He has something new for you.

February 17

The LORD created me at the beginning of
        his work,
    the first of his acts of long ago (Prov 8:22).

[Mary] is the bride of the Spirit, the mother of
the Son, the daughter of the Father on whom her
immaculate heart was forever centered. Let her go
with you before the Holy Trinity to whom you
belong, free though you are.

*Imagine Mary introducing you to the Spirit,
to her Son, to the Father.*

February 18

Do not be conquered by evil but conquer evil with good (Rom 12:21).

So many things are invisible to you. They emanate from your actions like a healing aureole. You know how evil tends to spread and gain ground? Then why should I not give love the blessed and all-victorious wings of light. Who can stop the flight of good from soul to soul right to the very end of the world?

Ask Jesus to show you how He sees healing and peace radiating from you.

February 19

For the love of Christ impels us, once we have come to the conviction that one died for all; therefore, all have died (2 Cor 5:14).

Let everything you do celebrate love. That will console Me for many others who pass Me by. Love alone can comfort love.

When you realize that you are able to console Him, what stirs within you? Express this to Him.

February 20

O God, you are my God, I seek you,
    my soul thirsts for you (Ps 63:1).

Even in your thoughts you should seek Me mostly and yourself very little. . . . Be like those who have their feet on earth but who talk to Me with their heads and hearts. Don't have any earthly cares. Live in Me and be concerned for My glory and whatever concerns love.

What would it look like for you to live this way—in Him and for Him?

February 21

Like living stones, let yourselves be built into a spiritual house, to be a holy priesthood, to offer spiritual sacrifices acceptable to God through Jesus Christ (1 Pet 2:5).

Do you realize how many sinners you can save in a single day? Think of My dazzling power, riches, and generosity. Who could hinder Me from giving you souls if I wish to do so?

Express to Jesus your gratitude for all He wants to do through you.

February 22

Jesus said to Simon Peter, "Simon son of John, do you love me more than these?" He said to him, "Yes, Lord; you know that I love you" (Jn 21:15).

But at least remember this: a word of love pays Me. And when you bring your lives close to My life and to heaven and the Eucharist, I cannot but carry you in My arms and cover you with My merits.

What moves in your heart as you listen to Jesus say these words to you?

February 23

The LORD will guide you continually,
and satisfy your needs in parched places,
and make your bones strong;
and you shall be like a watered garden,
like a spring of water,
whose waters never fail (Isa 58:11).

You don't take a single step without Me. How could you ever think that you are alone? I'm guiding every detail of your life. Let yourself be taken captive by My heart.

Where in your life do you feel most alone right now? Make an act of faith in Jesus, who guides every detail of your life.

February 24

O LORD, you will hear the desire of the meek;
you will strengthen their heart, you will
incline your ear (Ps 10:17).

Give Me everything that you blame in yourself,
since I am the one who transforms even the ugli-
est, the lowest, the most vile. I transmute everything into the gold of My glory. How can this be
done? By love.

*Ask Jesus to accomplish this transformation in
you.*

February 25

Have among yourselves the same attitude that is also yours in Christ Jesus,

Who, though he was in the form of God,
did not regard equality with God something to be grasped.
Rather, he emptied himself,
taking the form of a slave,
coming in human likeness (Phil 2:5–7).

Why be complicated? Respond to the simplicity of your Lord, and come every moment, unceasingly. Have you discovered what hinders you from coming?

Talk to Jesus simply, as you would a very trusted friend, about whatever is in your heart.

February 26

[The LORD] restores my soul.
He leads me in right paths
for his name's sake (Ps 23:3).

From now on, ask Me in your Communion to atone for any way in which you have grieved Me in your past life. When you receive Me like this, I penetrate every part of you, . . . and I restore you according to your wish.

Thank Jesus for this promise to permeate every part of your life and restore it to wholeness.

February 27

"Come, you that are blessed by my Father, inherit the kingdom prepared for you from the foundation of the world; for I was hungry and you gave me food" (Mt 25:34–35).

Remember that love is not puffed up with pride and that it will never pass away. What you do for yourself will perish miserably. What you do for others, for the love of Me, will go on re-echoing throughout all eternity.

Have you considered that what you have done for others will last for eternity?

February 28

For as a young man marries a young woman,
   so shall your builder marry you,
and as the bridegroom rejoices over the bride,
   so shall your God rejoice over you
      (Isa 62:5).

Will you at last believe in My love? Very simply,
every moment, no matter what happens? And
with the greatest joy?

*Imagine Jesus rejoicing over you at every stage
of your life. Share with Him how this makes
you feel about yourself, and about Him.*

February 29

The beloved of the LORD rests in safety—
the High God surrounds him all day long—
the beloved rests between his shoulders
(Deut 33:12).

Your beloved does so much for you. When you are absorbed in other things He is there. When you are putting forth great efforts because your faith is dim, He is there. When you no longer feel His presence, He is with you. And when you think you are deserted, He is right in your very center, alive, watchful, loving.

What stirs in your heart when you listen to these words?

MARCH

March 1

At an acceptable time, O God,
in the abundance of your steadfast love,
    answer me (Ps 69:13).

Aren't you beginning to understand that the words of your prayers have been shaped like arrows, not to beat the air, but to go straight to the heart of the Father who receives them with love? Every prayer has its arrow. Be certain of receiving an answer. . . . If He doesn't give you the answer you were hoping to get, it will be another—a better one.

Ask Jesus about prayers for which you are awaiting an answer.

March 2

"I have eagerly desired to eat this Passover with you before I suffer" (Lk 22:15).

I burned with desire to belong to all of you, to remain in your possession right to the end of time, to be something you could take, eat, and drink. To be shut into your church to wait for you there, to listen to you, to console you in the most intimate union of all. Won't you love Me more for that? What language must I speak to make you understand Me?

Listen in silence to these desires of His heart.

March 3

[Y]ou are precious in my sight,
and honored, and I love you (Isa 43:4).

Which of us is waiting the more impatiently for the moment of intimacy, you or I? Yes, I know that you are thinking about it and preparing for it, that you are coming out of a sense of duty. But I'm coming from pure love.

Let this really sink in: He can never be outdone in love. He has been waiting for this moment of prayer.

March 4

Then Jesus called the twelve together and gave them power and authority over all demons and to cure diseases, and he sent them out to proclaim the kingdom of God and to heal (Lk 9:1–2).

If you could only heal the wounds of those who come near you! Ask Me for this. Ask My mother. My little girl, so dear, so dear, will you let Me live again on earth in you?

Ask for the grace to be a healing presence—to bring Him to all you meet.

March 5

Your every act should be done with love (1 Cor 16:14).

I never force, even with regard to My gifts. You are free to take or leave them. How often your freedom has crucified Me! And so, I wait . . . I wait for centuries. Don't you realize that I've been waiting a long, long time for you? No two souls are alike. None other can give Me what I expect from you.

What does it mean when someone is willing to wait for you?

March 6

Your Maker is your husband,
    the LORD of hosts is his name;
the Holy One of Israel is your Redeemer,
    the God of the whole earth he is called
        (Isa 54:5).

If you could only see Me as I really am, what would you not do! You would throw yourself at My feet. You would hold Me to your heart, thanking Me for My sufferings and My blessings. You would ask My forgiveness for your willful faults and tell Me again of your love.

Right now, imagine seeing Him as He is. What would you do?

March 7

For as Christ's sufferings overflow to us, so through Christ does our encouragement also overflow (2 Cor 1:5).

My child, can't you understand that the trials I send you are all made to measure, exactly fitted to your power to bear, favors that draw you nearer to your beloved. Thank Me for a little trial as though it were a flower placed with new tenderness on your heart by your Fiancé.

What would it be like to look at your trials this way?

March 8

"Truly I tell you, unless you change and become like children, you will never enter the kingdom of heaven. Whoever becomes humble like this child is the greatest in the kingdom of heaven"(Mt 18:3–4).

In our relationship don't be afraid of your little-ness, for this is what touches My compassionate heart. And don't have any fear of meeting Me too often, since I'd be happy if you never left Me.

Is there anything you are afraid of in your relationship with Him?

March 9

Steadfast love surrounds those who trust in the LORD (Ps 32:10).

This should be your one fixed desire: To live only for Me. Your life will be filled to the brim with good things. I've been waiting so long for the joy of giving you more. Help Me. Ask Me to do so.

What would it look like for you to live only for Him?

March 10

But may I never boast except in the cross of our Lord Jesus Christ (Gal 6:14).

I am always crucified before the Father, who sees all time in a single instant. I am always the Lamb of God who takes away the sins of the world. And since I am yours, why don't you offer Me more often to heaven from the depths of your heart?

What stirs in your heart when you hear Jesus say this?

March 11

"Very truly, I tell you, unless you eat the flesh of the Son of Man and drink his blood, you have no life in you" (Jn 6:53).

For love I gave myself into the hands of men who did with Me as they wished. Now, I give Myself up in the Eucharist, and once again you do with Me what you wish. This is for love too. Right to the end. Right to the end of time.

Thank Him for the precious gift of the Eucharist. Plan how you will receive Him in your next Holy Communion.

March 12

Is it nothing to you, all you who pass by?
    Look and see
if there is any sorrow like my sorrow . . .
    (Lam 1:12).

I am all innocence, yet I suffered everything imaginable. Wouldn't you like to suffer everything too, so that we might be more one than ever? Do you think we're close enough now? Wouldn't you love to come closer? Has your love said its last word?

How do you want to respond to His questions?

March 13

The LORD set his heart on you and chose you (Deut 7:7).

It's a strange thing, isn't it, that a creature can comfort his God. And yet this is a fact. My love reverses the roles, inventing a new way for people to reach Me, by allowing them to give Me a protecting tenderness. So great is My need of all your ways of loving, all your ways of being tender.

What comfort and tenderness do you want to give Him?

March 14

"Do not fear, only believe" (Mk 5:36).

You would need to know all the cruelty of My executioners to understand My courage sustained by My love. Yes, I loved you, each one of you, even to such suffering as that. Then don't ever doubt Me, for I am infinite.

Imagine being able to truly understand Jesus' love for you. Ask Him for this grace.

March 15

[M]y mouth praises you with joyful lips
when I think of you on my bed,
and meditate on you in the watches of the
night (Ps 63:5–6).

Keep watch on your thoughts; they control your
words and actions. Dwell upon My thoughts, so
full of kindness and compassion, and you will do
My deeds.

*Look at the day ahead and decide now how
and when you will call to mind His thoughts.*

March 16

None of us lives for oneself, and no one dies for oneself. For if we live, we live for the Lord, and if we die, we die for the Lord; so then, whether we live or die, we are the Lord's (Rom 14:7–8).

Be to others what I was. Be your Christ for others. Give yourself because I gave Myself. I am your reason for living; let this be enough.

Ask Jesus to show you how He gave Himself and how you can be like Him.

March 17

For to me life is Christ, and death is gain (Phil 1:21).

It is good for you to abandon yourself to My tenderness. Life or death, what does it matter? You are in My heart. You are in My will. It isn't enough just to accept; your acceptance must be charged with the utmost love.

Rest in His heart, knowing you are safe.

March 18

But I was like a gentle lamb
   led to the slaughter (Jer 11:19).

Can you understand My thirst for your awareness of Me, for your desire to be pleasing to Me, for your gratitude for My pitiable sufferings, your compassion for all the disgrace, the filth, and the hatred I received during the night before My crucifixion and on the morning of My death? And for the blows and the torture of My body and mind. Do you sometimes think of it?

Can you open your heart to Him?

March 19

Mary treasured all these words and pondered them in her heart (Lk 2:19).

Pray. Show an example of heartwarming love. You remember how good My mother and Saint Joseph were to all those who received them during their travels. Long afterward people remembered their visit. They left a wake of blessings all along their way.

Talk to Him about how you could leave blessings behind you today.

March 20

Let my prayer be counted as incense before
you,
and the lifting up of my hands as an
evening sacrifice (Ps 141:2).

Multiply your sacrifices. Two or three a day are
not many, but united with Mine—can you imagine what a fortune that would be? . . . To pray is
itself a sacrifice like the smoke rising toward heaven
from the holocaust.

*Have you considered the value your sacrifices
could have? Talk to Jesus about it.*

March 21

The message of the cross is foolishness to those who are perishing, but to us who are being saved it is the power of God (1 Cor 1:18).

Don't run away any more from what costs you something, and you will be among the happiest of people. Besides, I've done so much for you . . .

To not run away from what is painful or difficult—what would this look like for you? Ask Jesus to show you how.

March 22

I know your works; you are neither cold nor hot. I wish that you were either cold or hot. So, because you are lukewarm, and neither cold nor hot, I am about to spit you out of my mouth (Rev 3:15–16).

Don't see sins in what are only nature's weaknesses. What makes Me suffer is indifference.

Jesus knows well the weakness of our human nature. How do you want to respond to His words?

March 23

Love is patient, love is kind. It is not jealous, [love] is not pompous, it is not inflated, it is not rude (1 Cor 13:4–5).

Do you know when you speak like Me? When you put goodness and charm into your words. When you touch hearts. When you give a gracious answer to an acid remark. When you make excuses for someone. When you serve. When you give. When you calm an angry person. When you comfort.

Look at the day ahead with Him and ask for the grace to speak like Him.

March 24

"I was hungry and you gave me food, I was thirsty and you gave me something to drink, I was a stranger and you welcomed me" (Mt 25:35).

You remember My words, "I thirst"? I am always thirsty. If you knew this thirst, more intense than [human] thirst, you would devise every means in your power to quench it. That is why I knock at your door.

What do you feel drawn to say to Jesus?

March 25

Mary said, "Here am I, the servant of the Lord; let it be with me according to your word" (Lk 1:38).

My mother lived for God alone. There was no selfishness in her, no egotism. Her life was a perfect response to the purpose for which the Creator had fashioned her. Imitate her.

Imagine what it would be like to begin imitating Mary. Decide how you can start today.

March 26

Not that of ourselves we are qualified to take credit for anything as coming from us; rather, our qualification comes from God (2 Cor 3:5).

Hasn't it ever occurred to you that this or that grace was given to you because of some prayer said for you, or some priest's blessing, or what your parents won by their efforts, or because of My divine compassion, or the goodness of My mother? Don't ever get the idea that the cause is any goodness of your own.

Thank God for all the people in your life who have been a channel for God's grace.

March 27

This saying is trustworthy and deserves full acceptance: Christ Jesus came into the world to save sinners. Of these I am the foremost (1 Tim 1:15).

From now on, won't everything in you be love—above all, your sorrow for your sins? Use your faults as a springboard to love Me better. And don't think this is a small thing. Love is never small.

What would it be like for you to use your faults as a springboard to love?

March 28

I urge you therefore, brothers, by the mercies of God, to offer your bodies as a living sacrifice, holy and pleasing to God, your spiritual worship (Rom 12:1).

Take your memory in your hands and offer it to Me. Do the same with each one of your faculties. In life we always have an inner store of little worries and difficulties that can be used to make amends for our sins and the sins of others.

What stirs in your heart when Jesus says this to you?

March 29

If, then, we have died with Christ, we believe that we shall also live with him (Rom 6:8).

As you gaze on Me you will understand that the suffering that passes leads to life eternal, and you will say, "How simple it is!" . . . You will say, "You were nothing but goodness and mercy and I didn't know it." Then the veil will be rent and you will have the face-to-face vision of all that I suffered for you.

Have you considered how different things will look from the point of view of heaven?

March 30

Rejoice insofar as you are sharing Christ's sufferings, so that you may also be glad and shout for joy when his glory is revealed (1 Pet 4:13).

Do something to atone for your self-love and the self-love of others. To make amends should be joyous, you know, since it heals and since it is for love. It is sin that is sad—the continual tendency to self-love that often makes you forget your God.

What is Jesus personally inviting you to?

March 31

Rejoice in hope, endure in affliction, persevere in prayer (Rom 12:12).

Trust yourself to My eyes; they see what you cannot see. Let your intention be to serve My intentions. And this will give you the courage to suffer. My little one, ask Me for this courage. It is always a feast day for Me when you ask Me for something—the beautiful feast of giving you My help.

Give Him the joy of asking for His help.

APRIL

April 1

"As the Father has loved me, so I have loved you; abide in my love" (Jn 15:9).

Nothing that you may possibly have imagined of the love of My heart comes anywhere near the reality. Remember that I wanted your joy so much that I came down to earth to know suffering.

When Jesus says His love is more than you can possibly imagine, what stirs in your heart?

April 2

"For where your treasure is, there your heart will be also" (Mt 6:21).

Today may I express a desire—you're listening? I should like you to acquire the habit of seeing Me in everyone, in the little daily incidents too. To see Me everywhere would be to think of your Savior always.

How can you respond to this call to see things anew?

April 3

O give thanks to the LORD, for he is good;
 for his steadfast love endures forever.
Let the redeemed of the LORD say so,
 those he redeemed from trouble
  (Ps 107:1–2).

Never will your thanks be filled with as much love and joy as I had in suffering to save you.

Thank Him with as much joy and love as you can.

April 4

Standing near the cross of Jesus were his mother, and his mother's sister, Mary the wife of Clopas, and Mary Magdalene (Jn 19:25).

Would you like to try to remain with Me, like Magdalene, with My mother? I want you to think only of Me, suffering for you, and I want you to seek ways of consoling Me.

What is Jesus calling you to? How could you console Him?

April 5

[L]ay aside every weight and the sin that clings so closely, and let us run with perseverance the race that is set before us, looking to Jesus the pioneer and perfecter of our faith (Heb 12:1–2).

Let Me come in and take over everything. Give yourself to Me. Don't let anything in you hinder Me from working through you.

What would it look like for you to let Him come in and work through you?

April 6

I am my beloved's and my beloved is mine (Song 6:3).

So don't be upset by anything. Once and for all, place your heart in Mine, in joy as in distress. If I fill your cup to overflowing, I am your peace. If I put you to the test, I am your companion. Nothing ever ceases to flow from Me to you, if you accept Me.

Read this over a few times. What is moving in your heart?

April 7

I will not forget you.
See, I have inscribed you on the palms of my
  hands (Isa 49:15–16).

Oh, be attentive to Me! This is a signal way of reaching Me. To be attentive means to empty yourself of everything except the desire for Me. It is then that I come, and the greater your desire for Me, the greater will be the measure of My grace.

Decide now to put your attention on Jesus instead of on negative thoughts.

April 8

The cup of blessing that we bless, is it not a participation in the blood of Christ? The bread that we break, is it not a participation in the body of Christ? (1 Cor 10:16).

Hide Me in your heart as though in this way you could save Me from wounding insults. For I receive them, above all in My Holy Eucharist. There, in your heart, thank Me, adore and console Me.

When you realize Jesus is asking for your tenderness, what stirs in your heart?

April 9

The meek shall obtain fresh joy in the LORD,
and the neediest people shall exult in the
Holy One of Israel (Isa 29:19).

When the love of the cross sinks deep into a person, he lives in a joy that the world can never know. For the world has only pleasures, but joy belongs to Me and Mine, My friend.

Ask Jesus about His joy and listen to what He wants to tell you.

April 10

"Those who eat my flesh and drink my blood abide in me, and I in them" (Jn 6:56).

One thing only I ask of you: oneness with Me. Since we are united in the morning in My Eucharist, let us not be separated by your indifference; it leads to constant mind-wandering. When people are in love they never stop thinking of the beloved, do they? Then what should I conclude if you don't think of Me?

Imagine what it would be like to have this oneness with Jesus.

April 11

He indeed died for all, so that those who live might no longer live for themselves but for him who for their sake died and was raised (2 Cor 5:15).

Never drink your cup of pleasure to the last drop. Keep a little for Me as a sacrifice—My part—you understand what I mean? Since in secret we are together in everything. If you took it all, what would I have?

When you read this, what do you feel called to do for Him?

April 12

"The Father himself loves you, because you have loved me" (Jn 16:27).

The grace of God—this beautiful, this wondrous grace—is never withheld from those who, through the instrumentality of someone (it could be you if you wish), leave behind their usual indifference and begin to aspire to greater intimacy with their Savior.

Do you desire intimacy with Jesus? What do you want to say to Him?

April 13

I am the bread that came down from heaven (Jn 6:41).

In the Host My heart is beating as it did on earth, as it does in heaven. There are not many hearts of Christ. There is only one. Believe without the shadow of a doubt in My Presence here before you and comfort Me by bringing your heart close to Mine.

Do you realize how close He desires to be with you?

April 14

For God so loved the world that he gave his only Son, so that everyone who believes in him may not perish but may have eternal life (Jn 3:16).

Do you know the outpouring of any love like His? A love as vehement, as faithful, as all-consuming, as full of delicate and incomparable sweetness. A love that is all readiness. This love is now. It is always now.

Marvel at God's love, and rest in it.

April 15

We know that all things work for good for those who love God, who are called according to his purpose (Rom 8:28).

You see that even your shortcomings can bring you closer to Me. Use them; you can transform them into the love that makes amends, the love of contrition. Everything should lead to love.

What would it look like for you to use your shortcomings to grow closer to Him?

April 16

"Be merciful, just as your Father is merciful" (Lk 6:36).

Today you wanted to live with My loving-kindness. Keep it by you all day long. Adore it. Love it. Let it be your very gentle companion, so that those around you feel the effects of it. Express it by smiles full of goodness. Try to judge no one today. Say all the good you can about others and don't mention their faults.

Look at the day ahead and decide how you will answer His call.

April 17

We love because he first loved us (1 Jn 4:19).

My love is beyond all your power to imagine. Your belief in this immensity of love that accompanies you is feeble because you judge your God according to [human] standards. But you, My child, at least you—surrender to me. Believe without trying to define.

How much love can you imagine? What would it be like for you to believe in His love?

April 18

What then shall we say to this? If God is for us, who can be against us? He who did not spare his own Son but handed him over for us all, how will he not also give us everything else along with him? (Rom 8:31–32).

Even if everything is dark in your heart, if My voice seems to have vanished forever, think: "He loves me and He gave Himself for me."

Read these lines over again. How do you desire to respond?

April 19

Whoever does good is from God (3 Jn 1:11).

Imitate Me as much as you are able. If you could only bring all the people around you to Me! Try to tell them that I love them and how much I love them. My love is so vehement that I'll forgive them everything from the moment they repent. Bring them to Me and I'll enfold you with them.

Ask for the grace to bring His love to everyone around you.

April 20

[T]his is the one to whom I will look,
    to the humble and contrite in spirit
        (Isa 66:2).

Remember that if the mighty ones of this world are honored with noisy eulogies and public fanfare, I am honored by the silent and attentive heart, by a delicate sacrifice known to no one, by a secret surrender, a tender inner glance.

What do you desire to give Jesus?

April 21

"My sheep hear my voice. I know them, and they follow me. I give them eternal life, and they will never perish. No one will snatch them out of my hand" (Jn 10:27–28).

You have experienced the delicate little touches of My tenderness and you've seen it also in the details of your life. For nothing is too small for my watchful love. You have learned to recognize Me in circumstances too. And this pleases Me so much.

Express your appreciation for His attentiveness.

April 22

Trust in the LORD, and do good (Ps 37:3).

Hunt for Me everywhere. I'll let Myself be captured with such joy. How could you expect to find Me if you didn't search? And when you have found Me, give Me to others. There are people I'm waiting to reach only through you. This is the mission foreseen for you from all eternity.

Decide right now to accept this mission.

April 23

More than that, I even consider everything as a loss because of the supreme good of knowing Christ Jesus my Lord (Phil 3:8).

Couldn't you put an end to all these little useless thoughts that do nothing for you or your neighbor or God, and substitute others of loving adoration, or desire for My kingdom, or zeal for the salvation of your brothers?

What would it look like for you to try what Jesus suggests?

April 24

Draw near to God, and he will draw near to you (Jas 4:8).

You remember how only Moses could approach God on Sinai. If anyone else crossed the borderline at the foot of the mountain he was struck dead. And now that the Son of God has come to die for His brothers, He says to you, "Draw near. Come, love Me without fear, for I love you."

What image comes to your mind? Show it to Jesus.

April 25

But may I never boast except in the cross of our Lord Jesus Christ, through which the world has been crucified to me, and I to the world (Gal 6:14).

Then give yourself in your wholeness to Me without ever taking yourself back. That means denying your preferences, wanting My joy and My kingdom of love. It means forgetting yourself and remembering Me—My being—not an exacting tyrant but a Lamb slain for love.

What is moving in your heart when you listen to His words?

April 26

The LORD, your God, is in your midst,
. . . he will rejoice over you with gladness,
   he will renew you in his love;
he will exult over you with loud singing
   (Zeph 3:17).

How easy to be joyous when you know that you are loved boundlessly by a good God. To know that you are happy about it would increase My own happiness.

Thank Jesus for His boundless love, and ask for a share in His joy.

April 27

"This is the bread that came down from heaven, not like that which your ancestors ate, and they died. But the one who eats this bread will live forever" (Jn 6:58).

My Eucharistic Presence is there every day, every night, among you. I'm there full of tenderness, rich with blessings for the taking.

When you realize the gift of Jesus' presence in the Blessed Sacrament, what stirs in your heart? Express your thoughts and feelings to Him.

April 28

You are my hiding place and my shield;
   I hope in your word (Ps 119:114).

Enter, enter into Me. What really counts is the life
of your soul, you understand? Everything should
be subservient to it. And the center of it should be
I, your Christ. All things uplifted to Me, everything for Me, since we are one as I and My Father
are one.

*What would it look like for you to make Jesus
the center of your life?*

April 29

I will sing of your might;
  I will sing aloud of your steadfast love in
    the morning (Ps 59:16).

Each day is a first creation. Not one is like another.
I never stop creating. And it is all for all of you. If I
didn't hold you up, you would cease to exist. Will
you love Me enough to thank Me for it?

*Decide right now to receive this new day as a
gift from God.*

April 30

Listen! my beloved is knocking.
"Open to me, my sister, my love,
    my dove, my perfect one" (Song 5:2).

Perhaps I created you only to console Me and to give Me a refuge in your heart where you sing Me the hymn of love. Why shouldn't I have a home on earth? Must I still have no stone on which to rest My head? Open to Me. Fling the doors of your heart wide open.

How do you feel called to respond to this invitation from Jesus?

MAY

May 1

"Do not be afraid, Mary, for you have found favor with God" (Lk 1:30).

Don't be astonished at My suggestion that you never cease asking for compassion, humility, and gentleness.... Wouldn't you be happier if you had these qualities? And isn't it always your happiness that I'm seeking?... Ask My mother to give them to you and offer sacrifices in exchange.

What stirs in you when you realize that Jesus links happiness with virtue?

May 2

But when the fullness of time had come, God sent his Son, born of a woman (Gal 4:4).

Live simply with us as at Nazareth. Nothing in our intimate life will be kept from you. I give everything I have, even the love of My mother. When you feel weak or alone, come to us. You don't need any introduction. We've known you for a long time and better than you know yourself.

Imagine yourself with the Holy Family at Nazareth and enjoy being with Jesus, Mary, and Joseph.

May 3

[Jesus] said to the disciple, "Here is your mother." And from that hour the disciple took her into his own home (Jn 19:27).

Who could be happier than you, My Christians? The same Father—Mine. The same mother—Mine. And I—your brother. Try to understand then, and be full of joy.

Sit for a while with this good news and notice what moves your heart.

May 4

Lo, this is our God; we have waited for him, so
   that he might save us.
This is the LORD for whom we have waited;
let us be glad and rejoice in his salvation
   (Isa 25:9).

I'm not just a Messenger of suffering as so many
imagine. I am also the Giver of joys and I love your
thanks, My little children; don't deprive Me of
this.

*Remember a joy Jesus gave you at some point
in your life. Express your thanks.*

May 5

Glory in his holy name;
    let the hearts of those who seek the LORD
        rejoice (Ps 105:3).

If you realize that your praise gives Me glory, you will praise Me better. Know that your love gives joy to My love; it's like two mirrors forever reflecting each other. Aren't you happy to think that you reflect your God? This God, so much yours that He wanted to create you in His image.

Have you considered the effect you can have on God?

May 6

Consider the generations of old and see:
> has anyone trusted in the Lord and been
> disappointed? . . .
Or has anyone called upon him and been
> neglected? (Sir 2:10).

Come closer, always closer. Give up everything that
separates us—the lack of confidence and hope. It
is a great thing to hope. Hope for holiness.

*How do you desire to respond to this call for
great confidence and hope?*

May 7

There is no fear in love, but perfect love casts out fear (1 Jn 4:18).

Don't ever give way to the distress that keeps you aloof from Me. Be sure that My goodness is infinitely greater than the sinfulness of My children. If you didn't count on Me for help, to whom would you turn? Hope and trust to the utmost in Me, and you will honor Me.

When you realize that God's goodness is greater than any human sin, what stirs in you?

May 8

May your soul rejoice in God's mercy,
and may you never be ashamed to praise
him (Sir 51:29).

If you can't keep your thoughts on Me, come back
to Me as soon as you notice this, gently, without
bitterness against yourself. Since I can put up with
you, you can surely put up with yourself. Transmute
this into an opportunity of being humble.

*How would it look for you to put up with
yourself gently?*

May 9

[May you be] strengthened with every power, in accord with his glorious might, for all endurance and patience, with joy, giving thanks to the Father, who has made you fit to share in the inheritance of the holy ones in light (Col 1:11–12).

You see that you can do nothing by yourself. Throw yourself into My arms every morning and ask Me for strength to pay attention to the little details.

Right now, ask for the grace you need to put all your trust in Jesus.

May 10

Trust in the LORD with all your heart,
 and do not rely on your own insight.
In all your ways acknowledge him,
 and he will make straight your paths
  (Prov 3:5–6).

Never be discouraged. Remind yourself often that I am with you. Can I be with you and not help you? Isn't the creature infinitely precious to the Creator? If you only knew!

What stirs in your heart as you read that you are infinitely precious to God, your Creator?

May 11

Do not let your hearts be troubled. Believe in God, believe also in me. In my Father's house there are many dwelling places. If it were not so, would I have told you that I go to prepare a place for you? (Jn 14:1–2).

Even if you loved Me each day with a heroic love, it would be so little compared with the love you will have for Me throughout all eternity.

Have you considered that what takes heroic effort now will be joyfully effortless in heaven?

May 12

Although you have not seen him, you love him; and even though you do not see him now, you believe in him and rejoice with an indescribable and glorious joy (1 Pet 1:8).

Do you believe in Me? Do you really believe in Me? Are you sure that I am in you, and that I loved you even to the folly of My cross?

Listen again to these words of Jesus. What do you think is in His heart, and how do you want to respond?

May 13

When Jesus saw his mother and the disciple whom he loved standing beside her, he said to his mother, "Woman, here is your son" (Jn 19:25–26).

Thank [Mary]. Love her. Above all, speak to her about your love, and this will draw you nearer to Me. Where else would she lead you if not to Me? She is much too humble to take for herself what belongs to Me, she who lived for God alone. Ask her to teach you to live for Me. Put all your trust in her.

Ask Mary to teach you what you feel you most need to know right now.

May 14

"The one who sent me is with me; he has not left me alone, for I always do what is pleasing to him" (Jn 8:29).

Don't refuse Me anything. Say: "My beloved, just as you wish." This will make Me happy, and the thought of My happiness will help you. Do your very utmost to be one with Me.

How do you desire to respond to Jesus? Talk to Him about it and ask for His help.

May 15

"And why has this happened to me, that the mother of my Lord comes to me? For as soon as I heard the sound of your greeting, the child in my womb leaped for joy" (Lk 1:43–44).

Ask My mother for the grace to live like her, in our company which is more real than all the visible world.

When you realize that there is an invisible world more real than the one that you see, what moves in your heart?

May 16

The angel said to her, "The Holy Spirit will come upon you, and the power of the Most High will overshadow you. . . . For nothing will be impossible with God" (Lk 1:35, 37).

Tell Him, the Spirit of love, to speak for you. Don't you think that it will be in the simplest, most delicate way? For the Spirit also adopts the language of the little ones. Wasn't My very humble mother overshadowed by Him when she answered the angel, "the handmaid of the Lord"?

Right now, ask the Holy Spirit to speak for you and to you. Then listen in silence.

May 17

"Give alms from your possessions, and do not let your eye begrudge the gift when you make it. Do not turn your face away from anyone who is poor, and the face of God will not be turned away from you" (Tob 4:7).

Let the compassion of My heart flow through you to all who come near you. Let them see it in your smile, in your way of welcoming them.

Decide to let Jesus' compassion flow through you today, realizing that it will be His love that does the work; you don't need to be able to do it.

May 18

I have been crucified with Christ; yet I live, no longer I, but Christ lives in me (Gal 2:19–20).

When I see you suffer, and suffer for Me, I gather each of your sufferings with great love, as though yours were greater than Mine, and had a value that My heart would like to make infinite. And this is why, when you allow Me to do so, I merge your life with Mine.

What moves in your heart when you hear Him say this to you?

May 19

There are others who are slow and need help,
    who lack strength and abound in poverty;
but the eyes of the Lord look kindly upon
        them;
    he lifts them out of their lowly condition
      (Sir 11:12).

There are the weaknesses of your nature, of course; sometimes you are careless. I know all about this. But don't be afraid. I am your Creator, your Savior.

*Have you considered that Jesus, our Savior,
understands the weaknesses of human nature?
Talk to Him about what is in your heart.*

May 20

"I say to you, Ask, and it will be given you; search, and you will find; knock, and the door will be opened for you" (Lk 11:9).

You don't ask Me for enough. Why are you so timid? Why don't I hear your voice? Don't you yet understand the joy I have in making your cup run over? But even if you don't understand, try to go deeper into the reality.

Give Him this joy: ask for more than you have dared to ask before.

May 21

Live in love, as Christ loved us and handed himself over for us as a sacrificial offering to God for a fragrant aroma (Eph 5:2).

Love is not selfish. Love never calculates. It hastens to help. In heaven there is nothing but love. And I bring it to the earth, whereas the Evil one sows hatred. There are two camps—choose. And if you choose love, don't remain shy and on the outskirts, as it were. Enter into the arena with the strong ones.

Choose love boldly today!

May 22

Be on your guard, stand firm in the faith, be courageous, be strong. Your every act should be done with love (1 Cor 16:13–14).

Give everything to love; and aim at perfection in all your work in order to please Me more and to make up for past flaws. Do you realize that a single one of such moments can make amends for an entire life?

What moves in your heart when you consider the power that a single moment of love can have?

May 23

"When you are praying, do not heap up empty phrases as the Gentiles do; for they think that they will be heard because of their many words" (Mt 6:7).

Don't aim at saying an exact number of wordy prayers. Just love Me simply. A look of your heart. The tender smile of a friend.

Right now, just look at Jesus and let Him look at you. Smile at Him as you would at a friend.

May 24

The prayer of the poor goes from their lips to the ears of God (Sir 21:5).

You've noticed, haven't you, that it's not so much what you say as the way you say it that gives weight to your remarks. It's like that when you talk to Me. So discover the loving way within you, the delicate shade of trust—and I'm vanquished. Since you know what your special weapons are, why not use these instead of any others?

What is Jesus hoping for from you?

May 25

Know the love of Christ that surpasses knowledge, so that you may be filled with all the fullness of God (Eph 3:19).

You know all about the redemption and the passion, but can you understand the love of your God—the feeling of this heart? Its intense desire is beyond your power to comprehend. Repeat to yourself often, "I believe in Your love for me, in Your boundless love. I know that you have loved me with an everlasting love."

Pray this prayer, looking at a crucifix.

May 26

[I]t was I who taught Ephraim to walk,
   I took them up in my arms;
   but they did not know that I healed them
   (Hos 11:3).

Don't you have the impression that you still think of Me as being the distant and severe one? Smile when you speak to Me, believing that this makes Me happy. And if you think of the joy you give Me, won't you come closer and more happily to Me, as though you were in My heart?

*What image comes to mind when Jesus speaks
of the joy you give Him?*

May 27

"Father, I desire that those also, whom you have given me, may be with me where I am, to see my glory, which you have given me because you loved me before the foundation of the world" (Jn 17:24).

And how can My joy be described? The joy of your Christ who yearns so much for oneness with His children that He invented the Eucharist in order to merge with them.

Express your gratitude to Jesus for the gift of the Eucharist, and ask for the grace of this oneness with Him.

May 28

"Give us this bread always" (Jn 6:34).

You receive Me in your Communion in the morning. What is there to prevent you from giving thanks all day long? You want to love Me in all circumstances, but you are in the world and surrounded by others. Then you can continue to love Me in this one and that one, can't you? What keeps you from doing this?

Plan to love Jesus in each person you meet today.

May 29

All these were constantly devoting themselves to prayer, together with certain women, including Mary the mother of Jesus, as well as his brothers (Acts 1:14).

Never stop asking that the Spirit of holiness, the Holy Spirit, may come and take possession of you. Ask this through the one He covered with His shadow, My mother, your mother.

Ask Mary to show you how to open yourself more to the working of the Holy Spirit.

May 30

"And blessed is she who believed that there would be a fulfillment of what was spoken to her by the Lord" (Lk 1:45).

Show Me your inadequacies, especially the most discouraging ones, such as your lack of perseverance in keeping watch on your bad habit. . . . Take My mother into your confidence. She'll help you keep watch. It will be easier with both of you, won't it?

What would it look like for you to take Mary into your confidence?

May 31

"Hail Mary, full of grace, the Lord is with you; blessed are you among women" (cf. Lk 1:28).

Let us include My mother in this life of ours. Do you really believe that her love is active on your behalf? Oh, My little girl, have faith in the great things that you can do with us. Without us . . . but you are already aware of your nothingness.

When you realize that Mary is active on your behalf, what stirs in your heart?

JUNE

June 1

"Come to me, all you that are weary and are carrying heavy burdens, and I will give you rest" (Mt 11:28).

Y ou remember in the gospel it is written that only to touch the hem of My robe brought healing. And you feed upon Me; you possess Me utterly. What is not My power in you to heal you, change you, completely transform you in a single instant? Believe that. Do you really believe it?

Right now, decide to ask with faith for the healing you need.

June 2

When he was at the table with them, he took bread, blessed and broke it, and gave it to them. Then their eyes were opened, and they recognized him (Lk 24:30–31).

Just think what it means to receive Communion. How heartless not to say thank you! I gave all of Myself to My little children. Whoever wants Me may take Me. And those who receive, receive all heaven, for heaven is your Christ.

Looking forward to your next Holy Communion, what do you feel drawn to say to Jesus?

June 3

It was not because you were more numerous than any other people that the LORD set his heart on you and chose you—for you were the fewest of all peoples. It was because the LORD loved you (Deut 7:7–8).

It's because you are smaller and weaker than others that I've chosen you. Be one with Me as you suffer in your body; as though I had been mocked and scourged this morning.

What would it be like for you to see your weaknesses and physical problems as a way of being closer to Him?

June 4

Having loved his own who were in the world, he loved them to the end (Jn 13:1).

Offer this communion between us to the Father in union with the communion between the three divine persons. After you receive the Eucharist, offer Him not only My body, but the perfections of My soul: My power and My tenderness; My virtues, too—the ones you have loved the best—in order to help you to overcome your weaknesses and failures.

Ask Jesus about the "communion" He mentions here.

June 5

I have loved you with an everlasting love;
therefore I have continued my faithfulness
to you (Jer 31:3).

Don't let a day go by without doing something
for Me, for there is not a single day when I am not
at work in you for your own happiness. Do you
believe Me?

*Reflect on all He is doing for you today. What
do you desire to do for Him?*

June 6

Let me see your face,
    let me hear your voice;
for your voice is sweet,
    and your face is lovely (Song 2:14).

Is it because I'm God that you think I have no need of tenderness? Do you think I remain silent with those who want to talk with Me? Talk with Me ...

What stirs in your heart when you read this? Talk to Him tenderly.

June 7

Let what you heard from the beginning abide in you. If what you heard from the beginning abides in you, then you will abide in the Son and in the Father (1 Jn 2:24).

I do more than visit you. I in-dwell you. You partake of Me as food. I never leave you unless you drive Me away. Then find within you heart-melting words of love.

How can you respond to Jesus? Ask Him to help you understand this in-dwelling.

June 8

The steadfast love of the LORD never ceases,
    his mercies never come to an end;
they are new every morning;
    great is your faithfulness (Lam 3:22–23).

Sometimes you say, "If only one could have several lives!" Instead of that, every morning awaken to the thought that a new life is given to you, and make better use of it than yesterday.

What would it look like for you to awaken every morning with this thought and resolve?

June 9

A woman in the crowd raised her voice and said to him, "Blessed is the womb that bore you and the breasts that nursed you!" But he said, "Blessed rather are those who hear the word of God and obey it" (Lk 11:27–28).

You know, on earth the tenderness between My mother and Me was so great that we had only one heart. Try to be like her by making your will one with Mine, your great friend.

Ask Mary, the mother of Jesus, to show you how to have one heart with Jesus.

June 10

For we are his handiwork, created in Christ Jesus for the good works that God has prepared in advance, that we should live in them (Eph 2:10).

Love Me, love intensely. You can never know all that you can obtain and transform with your love on earth. But I know.

What do you feel drawn to say to Jesus? Express what is in your heart when you read this.

June 11

Let your speech always be gracious, seasoned with salt, so that you know how you should respond to each one (Col 4:6).

It is through you that I am speaking to this one and that one to bring them cheer and encourage them to come close to Me and talk to Me about themselves. I should so love to have their confidence. Never mind if they don't know how to speak to Me, these poor people—I want them to come without any fear.

How can you allow Him to speak today, through you?

June 12

"I will do whatever you ask in my name, so that the Father may be glorified in the Son" (Jn 14:13).

If you hope in My love, you will no longer count on yourself. You will expect My help in every difficult situation. You will think, "I can't do anything, but there is nothing the beloved can't do." And full of trust and peace you will take up your task of love again, happy to toil day and night to console Me.

What would life be like for you if you increased your trust in this way?

June 13

[May you] have strength to comprehend with all the holy ones what is the breadth and length and height and depth, and to know the love of Christ that surpasses knowledge, so that you may be filled with all the fullness of God (Eph 3:18–19).

Consider the height—the greatness of the gift. The depth—God himself. The "breadth—the gift for everyone" in My Eucharist. And bring others to It.

What image comes to your mind when you consider the gift of the Eucharist? Share it with Jesus.

June 14

Let us hold fast to the confession of our hope without wavering, for he who has promised is faithful (Heb 10:23).

Fan the flame of your confidence. Don't you need it along your way? Keep it burning in Me. I want you to be happy, so come back again and again to this feeling of trust until you are never without it.

What fans the flame of your trust, and what smothers or erodes it? Speak to Jesus about this.

June 15

I am my beloved's and my beloved is mine;
  he pastures his flock among the lilies
    (Song 6:3).

You realize that I'm in you, don't you? And if you do, why don't you think of it more often? I was going to say "always." Then My longing for you would be completely satisfied.

How do you feel called to respond to Jesus' longing for you?

June 16

He rained down on them manna to eat,
and gave them the grain of heaven.
Mortals ate of the bread of angels;
he sent them food in abundance
(Ps 78:24–25).

Do you believe enough to find in each Eucharist the food that should strengthen your love? You know that this is all that counts: to make love grow in your heart.

Ask Jesus to strengthen your love and make it grow.

June 17

"Stay with us, because it is almost evening and the day is now nearly over" (Lk 24:29).

Perhaps you don't realize what joy My children's little visits give Me? Especially when they come to see Me and not the architecture or the beauties of the church. When they speak to Me as to a friend, not in recited prayers.

Can you imagine yourself stopping by the church for a visit when you're in the area?

June 18

"Blessed are the poor in spirit, for theirs is the kingdom of heaven" (Mt 5:3).

You know very well that I look at the soul's intent in every action rather than the action itself. What I want in you is a spirit of love and humility, one that is constant and independent of created things, freed from the earth and ready for heaven at my first call. Joyously ready.

What would it be like for you to have this spirit of love and freedom?

June 19

"If you keep my commandments, you will abide in my love, just as I have kept my Father's commandments and abide in his love" (Jn 15:10).

Give more importance to the little things. Some are so little that you often neglect to fill them with love. And yet, in My eyes, God's eyes, do you think there is a big difference between the small actions of your daily duty . . . and what you call the great events of your life?

Ask Him to explain to you how He sees the little things and big things of your life.

June 20

Those who are wise shall shine like the brightness of the sky, and those who lead many to righteousness, like the stars forever and ever (Dan 12:3).

I walk along the same path with you, the path that I chose for you from all eternity—in this family, in this country where you live. It is I who placed you there with a special love. So live there, full of faith, remembering that there is where you will win heaven.

Thank God for the path He has chosen for you.

June 21

As a deer longs for flowing streams,
  so my soul longs for you, O God.
My soul thirsts for God,
  for the living God.
When shall I come and behold
  the face of God? (Ps 42:1–2).

When you don't go deep into the inner stillness you deprive Me.

Read these words of Jesus over again. What stirs in your heart? Talk to Him about it.

June 22

Therefore, since we are surrounded by so great a cloud of witnesses, let us also lay aside every weight and the sin that clings so closely, and let us run with perseverance the race that is set before us (Heb 12:1).

In your desire to be one with Me, join more often with the saints on earth and the saints in heaven. You will be stronger; alone, you are so little.

Who are the saints on earth you can join with? Which heavenly friends can you turn to for strength?

June 23

I know, O LORD, that the way of human
    beings is not in their control,
        that mortals as they walk cannot direct
        their steps (Jer 10:23).

Don't worry. Since you can't do anything about
these things, you don't need to bother about them;
they're My concern. Just put them in My hands,
and that's all that matters.

*Imagine Him right there in front of you, and
place all your worries in His hands one by one,
and let Him carry them.*

June 24

For we do not have a high priest who is unable to sympathize with our weaknesses, but we have one who in every respect has been tested as we are, yet without sin (Heb 4:15).

Oh, yes, be full of joy. Do you know what the world was like before I came? There was God and there were men. Now God has become a man among men—one of you. What love!

Thank the Father for sending His Son, who understands all we go through because He is human like us.

June 25

He has shown strength with his arm;
    he has scattered the proud in the thoughts
        of their hearts.
He has brought down the powerful from their
    thrones,
        and lifted up the lowly (Lk 1:51–52).

Get a true picture of yourself in all your weakness, without even the possibility of being good without Me. But in the distress of your poverty, look at all My riches: they are all yours. Look at My goodness and throw yourself into My arms.

Ask for both humility and trust—especially whichever one is more difficult for you.

June 26

"Let it be known to all of you, and to all the people of Israel, that this man is standing before you in good health by the name of Jesus Christ of Nazareth, whom you crucified, whom God raised from the dead" (Acts 4:10).

See that you mention My name often in your conversations. You did this today, didn't you, and you noticed that it was like sunlight. It was so simple and yet so deep. Above all, don't count on yourself; count on Me in you.

What would it be like for you to mention Jesus more often in conversation?

June 27

After you have suffered for a little while, the God of all grace, who has called you to his eternal glory in Christ, will himself restore, support, strengthen, and establish you (1 Pet 5:10).

Keep in mind this prayer, "Lord, deliver me from anxiety about trifles!" Everything is insignificant apart from God whose life in you should daily seek to increase. In the next life you will ask yourself, "How could I ever remain a single instant without loving Him?"

Consider what is truly most important in your life.

June 28

A glad heart makes a cheerful countenance (Prov 15:13).

Don't you find that the inward smiles I've asked for and that you give Me make your life joyous? And don't you think that your neighbor will notice this radiant peace and find comfort in it? A personal grace very rarely fails to brim over to everyone.

Decide now to smile inwardly at Jesus whenever you think of Him today.

June 29

You came near when I called on you;
  you said, "Do not fear!" (Lam 3:57).

Don't be discouraged. There are many ways of advancing, even by your stumblings. Call out to Me. Don't be afraid to cry if you fall. But let your cry go straight to your matchless friend. Believe in My power. Didn't I catch hold of Peter when he was sinking beneath the waves? And don't you think I'm more ready to help you than to lose you?

How do you want to respond to these words of Jesus?

June 30

[Christ] chose us in him, before the foundation of the world, to be holy and without blemish before him. In love he destined us for adoption to himself through Jesus Christ (Eph 1:4–5).

Don't be afraid to offer yourself to the fulfillment of My dream of you, as though I were waiting to be encouraged by your burning desires. Say, "Lord, make me what You wanted me to be."

Pray this prayer right now. What desire stirs in your heart?

JULY

July 1

"Very truly, I tell you, if you ask anything of the Father in my name, he will give it to you. Until now you have not asked for anything in my name. Ask and you will receive, so that your joy may be complete" (Jn 16:23–24).

When will you do Me the honor of expecting from Me much more than you ever ask or think? Since I am all-Power and since I love you.

Imagine what it would be like to expect from Jesus more than you have ever expected before.

July 2

I am continually with you;
    you hold my right hand. . . .
Whom have I in heaven but you?
    And there is nothing on earth that I desire
        other than you (Ps 73:23, 25).

As the hunter cautiously and silently approaches his prey, close in on your remembrance of God. Silence your memory of the earth and let your prayer fly straight upward. I, your Lord, tell you this. I shall not resist the arrows that you shoot with all the strength of your will.

How do you feel drawn to respond to this invitation?

July 3

I will lead the blind
    by a road they do not know, . . .
I will turn the darkness before them into light,
    the rough places into level ground.
These are the things I will do,
    and I will not forsake them (Isa 42:16).

Get used to walking in the dark like the blind.
Trusting My hand to guide you. You couldn't
insult My heart more than to doubt it.

Consider how much Jesus desires your trust.
What moves in your heart?

July 4

For you were called for freedom, brothers. But do not use this freedom as an opportunity for the flesh; rather, serve one another through love (Gal 5:13).

Think often about Me, My little girl. Think often. With so little you give Me so much joy. Your free will with all its opportunities will no longer exist in heaven, you understand? Here you may choose; you may be for yourself or for Me.

Ask Him to help you see all the opportunities today to choose Him.

July 5

"My grace is sufficient for you, for power is made perfect in weakness." I will rather boast most gladly of my weaknesses, in order that the power of Christ may dwell with me (2 Cor 12:9).

Close the eyes of this fear that paralyzes you and throw yourself into My arms. I am the very gentle Shepherd; you know that I'll give you rest on My heart.

Throw yourself on the gentle Shepherd's heart, and in that safe place, let go of any paralyzing fear you have.

July 6

"I am thirsty" (Jn 19:28).

Divine longing . . . how vehement it is! How far beyond thought! At least honor Me by acknowledging it. I am thirsty, do you understand what I mean? I am thirsty for you all. Let Me drink.

Ask Jesus about his longing. Tell Him you want to quench His thrist.

July 7

"My sheep hear my voice. I know them, and they follow me. I give them eternal life, and they will never perish. No one will snatch them out of my hand" (Jn 10:27–28).

Speak to Me, as it were, with smiles. So many people look upon Me as an executioner or an inexorable judge. My heart wants to be your gentle friend. What would I not do for those who really want to give themselves to Me in confident and childlike surrender!

Picture the most gentle person you know. Then reflect how Jesus is even more gentle with you.

July 8

When the poor and needy seek water,
    and there is none,
    and their tongue is parched with thirst,
I the LORD will answer them,
    I the God of Israel will not forsake them
        (Isa 41:17).

Dare to hope more than you have ever hoped before, as you come to believe in the divine open-handedness. We aren't on the same plane: then expect the extraordinary.

Today, dare to raise your expectations of Jesus and what He will give to you.

July 9

Now I rejoice in my sufferings for your sake, and in my flesh I am filling up what is lacking in the afflictions of Christ on behalf of his body, which is the church (Col 1:24).

Give Me your suffering. No one can give it to Me in heaven. Give it to Me.

Imagine holding your suffering in your hands. Ask Jesus in what way He wants you to give it to Him.

July 10

He has told you, O mortal, what is good;
    and what does the LORD require of you
but to do justice, and to love kindness,
    and to walk humbly with your God?
        (Mic 6:8).

I can sanctify you in an instant. But I love your long and patient work; it keeps you humble. Acquire loving humility—it will exalt you. Discouragement never elevates anyone.

What would it look like for you to let go of your discouragement and allow Jesus to change it to humility?

July 11

Through him the whole structure is held together and grows into a temple sacred in the Lord; in him you also are being built together into a dwelling place of God in the Spirit (Eph 2:21–22).

Believe in the effectiveness of your work as part of the universal work of the saints. Think of the "living stone" that you are adding to the spiritual house—this stone that no one else but you is called upon to place in just this same position. This ought to encourage you to make efforts of every kind.

With faith and trust, thank Jesus for your unique calling.

July 12

You gave your people food of angels,
and without their toil you supplied them from
   heaven with bread ready to eat,
providing every pleasure and suited to every
   taste (Wis 16:20).

Today's Communion is different from yesterday's
and tomorrow's; the grace I give is always unique.
God's love is infinite and creative.

Have you considered that each Holy Commu-
nion is an amazing and unrepeatable gift?

July 13

Do not work for the food that perishes, but for the food that endures for eternal life, which the Son of Man will give you. For it is on him that God the Father has set his seal" (Jn 6:27).

All day long remember that My body has lived in your body. Even your gestures will take on gentleness from this.

Imagine the gentleness of Jesus flowing through you. What would that look like in your daily life?

July 14

I will never leave you or forsake you (Heb 13:5).

You don't always feel Me in the same way, but don't let the darkness hinder you from going forward. Humble yourself and go on your way faithfully. Keep going. You don't see Me or feel Me, but I'm there—love itself, holding out My arms to you.

Ask Jesus for the gift of faithful perseverance.

July 15

"What eye has not seen, and ear has not heard, and what has not entered the human heart, what God has prepared for those who love him" (1 Cor 2:9).

Remember that you are one of My members and that in placing you on the earth, I have mapped out a path for you alone. Promise Me again to follow it as the one you cherish the most, since I planned it for you and because coming from Me it brings you to Me.

When Jesus speaks of His plan for you, what stirs in your heart?

July 16

Do not fear, or be afraid;
> have I not told you from of old and
> declared it?
> You are my witnesses!
> Is there any god besides me?
> There is no other rock; I know not one
> (Isa 44:8).

Look at Me. Do you trust Me? Do you hope in Me? Unwaveringly, unreservedly? The hope I want you to have transcends death, since I am all in all to you; haven't you told Me that?

Look at Jesus. How do you desire to respond to His questions?

July 17

We know that all things work for good for those who love God, who are called according to his purpose (Rom 8:28).

How much comfort people would find and what happiness even in the midst of trials, if they only believed that everything that happens to them comes from My desire to do them good and that all is fitted to the measure of each one.

Imagine having the faith that all is either willed or permitted by God.

July 18

"I was hungry and you gave me food, I was thirsty and you gave me something to drink, I was a stranger and you welcomed me, I was naked and you gave me clothing, I was sick and you took care of me, I was in prison and you visited me" (Mt 25:35–36).

When you help others, let it be for Me and not just for the satisfaction of being kind. Purify your look at Me. Make it keener. Do everything to assure our intimacy.

Have you considered that one can be kind for a flawed reason? Decide right now that all your kindness will be for Him.

July 19

Do not fear, for I have redeemed you;
  I have called you by name, you are mine
    (Isa 43:1).

You don't have enough trust. Who will give Me this look of abandonment that I'm waiting for? Keep in mind more often that I give you everything for nothing: all My heaven for your nothingness and for the mere pittance of your yearnings. Think of this more often so that your heart may be stirred.

What stirs in your heart at the thought that He gives you all of Himself?

July 20

But for me it is good to be near God;
　　I have made the Lord GOD my refuge,
　　to tell of all your works (Ps 73:28).

Sometimes you feel Me more, sometimes less, but I never change. Don't let praying tire you. Why do you give yourself so much trouble? Let it be utterly simple and heartwarming, a family chat.

What would experiencing prayer in a simpler way look like for you?

July 21

"I am the good shepherd. I know my own and my own know me, just as the Father knows me and I know the Father. And I lay down my life for the sheep" (Jn 10:14–15).

Why be so anxious about the opinion of others? Isn't Mine enough? If you are with Me, let them talk. Take your place on My shoulder and forget everything.

Make the decision to leave everything in the hands of Jesus today and not be anxious about people's opinions.

July 22

His mother said to the servants, "Do whatever he tells you" (Jn 2:5).

What you can't manage yourself—the control of your words, or the thought of My Presence—you will find easier with the help of My mother. Ask her to help you. I confided Mary Magdalene and the holy women to her. Be like them: don't leave her.

Decide now to allow Mary to help you manage things today.

July 23

"He has looked with favor on the lowliness of
his servant. . . .
From now on all generations will call me
blessed" (Lk 1:48).

I am here for you. For your littleness I have My
greatness and My power. Make use of your elder
brother. Above all, don't doubt. Seeing in the
dark—there is your victory! Being sure, with the
assurance of love.

*What stirs in your heart when you read that
Jesus is here for you?*

July 24

[W]ith the Lord one day is like a thousand years, and a thousand years are like one day. The Lord is not slow about his promise, as some think of slowness, but is patient with you (2 Pet 3:8–9).

A little more each day—ever so gently, without taxing your soul. More frequent holy desires. A little upsoaring of your heart to Me, an affectionate glance. Less time spent far from any remembrance of Me; a sunnier loyalty, a silence of humility; a kindness for My sake.

What "little more" can you gently do today?

July 25

Kindness is like a garden of blessings,
and almsgiving endures forever (Sir 40:17).

Work for your neighbor. You should love him as your own body and mind.... Don't you think that at least three quarters of the people who do wrong fell into their way of life because they were not loved enough? How much an affectionate look, an outstretched hand, might have done in this or that circumstance.

Be on the lookout today for someone who needs an outstretched hand.

July 26

You arose . . . as a mother in Israel (Judg 5:7).

All that a mother has also belongs to her children. Have you ever met a mother who refused to share? She gives you everything if you ask her. Everything! So grow rich through her, for My glory.

Jesus wants us to go to His mother, Mary, so talk with her about what you need.

July 27

For to you has been granted, for the sake of Christ, not only to believe in him but also to suffer for him (Phil 1:29).

Don't be surprised at having to suffer for Me or at being tested and tried for My sake. These are records to be filled out for eternity. You take your place in the sacrifice for which the crown is prepared. You play your part in the unfinished symphony of My passion.

Have you considered that your sufferings can be part of His unfinished symphony?

July 28

Do not . . . abandon that confidence of yours; it brings a great reward (Heb 10:35).

Poor little ones, you have such a false idea of your Savior. Do you think He would redeem you and then abandon you? Don't set limits to your confidence. He sets no limits to His favors. Hunger for God and you will receive. If you don't call Him, how can He come?

What idea do you have of your Savior, Jesus?

July 29

Have mercy on me, O God,
according to your steadfast love;
according to your abundant mercy
blot out my transgressions (Ps 51:3).

Never mind if you haven't kept your word, or if you have fallen lower than yesterday. If you despise yourself and tell Me so in sorrow, you needn't be afraid to believe that you are in My heart. This heart, so great and good, so little like the hearts of men.

When you realize that you are in His heart, what moves in yours?

July 30

When I found him whom my soul loves,
I held him, and would not let him go
  (see Song 3:4).

Don't offend Me by being afraid and running away. That's what hurts love. Enter into My immensity like a little child who joyously seeks to drink and sleep on its mother's breast. Rest. Take strength for yourself. Take joy. Everything is in Me. For you.

Rest with Jesus right now. Express your joy in Him.

July 31

Do not fear, for I am with you,
    do not be afraid, for I am your God;
I will strengthen you, I will help you,
    I will uphold you with my victorious right
        hand (Isa 41:10).

Nothing happens by itself. So never lose sight of My watchful, kindly providence. And thank Me for My invisible care. My love loves to plan for you and does everything for your good.

What would it look like for you to trust in the care and plan of Jesus for you?

AUGUST

August 1

I have loved you with an everlasting love;
   therefore I have continued my faithfulness
   to you (Jer 31:3).

Then don't be afraid to talk to Me about yourself,
to blossom in My sight, to let Me look at you just
as you are. Even though I know you, I like you to
express yourself. It creates new longings and desires
in you. You must have secrets to confide in Me.

Today, allow yourself to blossom in His sight.

August 2

Live in love, as Christ loved us and handed himself over for us as a sacrificial offering to God (Eph 5:2).

Tenderly offer your sacrifice for the world. Aren't there others weaker than you? Can they rise up without Me? If you wanted to save a person very dear to you and this beloved person refused your help, how much you would suffer! I want to help the world, and the world refuses My help.

What do you feel drawn to offer to Jesus today?

August 3

"The friend of the bridegroom, who stands and hears him, rejoices greatly at the bridegroom's voice. For this reason my joy has been fulfilled. He must increase, but I must decrease" (Jn 3:29–30).

Keep Me company more and more. You can never know what it means to Me to be treated as an intimate friend. It is so rare.

Express to Jesus what it means to you to be invited to His company.

August 4

He woke up and rebuked the wind, and said to the sea, "Peace! Be still!" Then the wind ceased, and there was a dead calm. He said to them, "Why are you afraid? Have you still no faith?" (Mk 4:39–40).

Get out of yourself. Surrender the helm of your life to Me. Let your soul be lost in Mine. Why do you want to do everything? Give Me your trust and then just let yourself drift along wherever I take you.

What would it look like for you to surrender your life to Jesus in this way?

August 5

Sing and rejoice, O daughter Zion! For lo, I will come and dwell in your midst, says the LORD (Zech 2:10).

When you approach Me, My little girl, be full of joy, like a happy child. You are thinking, "He's always asking me for inward smiles." Could you believe that even though I am God I need the smiles of My children, because your happiness is essential to Me? Who can comprehend this? Who can even bear such a thought? But believe.

How do you desire to respond to Jesus' request?

August 6

For God who said, "Let light shine out of darkness," has shone in our hearts to bring to light the knowledge of the glory of God on the face of [Jesus] Christ (2 Cor 4:6).

Be grateful when you are surprised by a sudden illumination. Welcome this light; make it your own. Follow its beam as far as it shines. It is a blessing from God. You are discovering His love.

Recall a past insight or moment of consolation and welcome its light again.

August 7

He was praying in a certain place, and after he had finished, one of his disciples said to him, "Lord, teach us to pray, as John taught his disciples" (Lk 11:1).

I transform your prayers into My prayers, but if you don't pray . . . Can I make a plant that you haven't sown bear blossoms?

What stirs in your heart when you read these words? Express to Jesus what it is that moves you.

August 8

On that day you will know that I am in my Father, and you in me, and I in you (Jn 14:20).

So don't do anything outside of Me. Even if you consider that it has nothing to do with Me. Everything has to do with Me. Don't shut Me out; never shut Me out.

When you realize Jesus' desire to be part of everything in your life, how do you want to respond?

August 9

Abide in me as I abide in you. Just as the branch cannot bear fruit by itself unless it abides in the vine, neither can you unless you abide in me (Jn 15:4).

Fix it firmly in your mind that this presence of Me in you is not an allegory or a fantasy or a metaphor. It's not a story you listen to or something that might have happened to someone else. It has to do with you and Me. It has to do with a reality to be lived.

What would it be like for you to truly believe in His presence in you?

August 10

I am content with weaknesses, insults, hardships, persecutions, and constraints, for the sake of Christ; for when I am weak, then I am strong (2 Cor 12:10).

Love grows by loving. Don't calculate; practice the direct outpouring of the heart whether you pray or thank, or whether you ask for My kingdom and My glory.

Ask Jesus for the grace to be able to love without calculating.

August 11

So, as you received Christ Jesus the Lord, walk in him, rooted in him and built upon him and established in the faith as you were taught, abounding in thanksgiving (Col 2:6–7).

Pull yourself up by the roots, and plant yourself in Me.

He wants to be the basis and foundation of your life, the soil for you to grow in. How will you respond?

August 12

By this everyone will know that you are my disciples, if you have love for one another (Jn 13:35).

Keep watch on your lower nature, the part that
runs down your neighbor made in My image. Give
the kind of affection that comforts. You know
what I mean—the word, the glance. I am in all
ways of loving, just as Satan is in all ways of wounding. You see the source? You see the fruit? Choose,
and always be ready to choose Me. This is what it is
to be always in love.

What do you feel drawn to choose today?

August 13

Do not let your hearts be troubled, and do not let them be afraid (Jn 14:27).

Above all, confidence! When you have an anxiety and you can do nothing about it, just think, "He will straighten that out for me"—and go back into the peace within Me.

Imagine how much less anxiety and how much more calm this would lead to in your life.

August 14

"The kingdom of heaven is like treasure hidden in a field, which someone found and hid; then in his joy he goes and sells all that he has and buys that field" (Mt 13:44).

Keep on exploring My hidden treasures. You can never come to the end of them. Discover, discover, until fires undreamed of are kindled within you.

Ask Him to reveal a little more of Himself to you today.

August 15

A great portent appeared in heaven: a woman clothed with the sun, with the moon under her feet, and on her head a crown of twelve stars (Rev 12:1).

Practice your faith. When you were learning to walk, you leaped forward at a venture, and little by little you became surefooted. Do the same in your inner life. Take a flying leap toward the Trinity, toward My mother, in upsoarings hitherto unknown to you, more direct, more sincere, impelled from the very center of your being.

Where in your life are you being invited to take a big leap forward?

August 16

Rejoice in hope, endure in affliction, persevere in prayer (Rom 12:12).

This is the test of your faithfulness to Me: When you are . . . occupied with your business affairs, give your whole attention to them. But during the hours of prayer and love, let nothing distract you from Me. You enter into Me; there you abide, looking after Me and My interests.

What would it look like for you to live this way?

August 17

Because your steadfast love is better than life,
   my lips will praise you.
So I will bless you as long as I live;
   I will lift up my hands and call on your
   name (Ps 63:3–4).

Would I ask every soul to be holy if it were not possible? Very well then, believe in My help. Call Me often, still more often. Don't be afraid of being too insistent.

What desire stirs in your heart when you read that Jesus wants you to ask His help insistently?

August 18

"Listen! I am standing at the door, knocking; if you hear my voice and open the door, I will come in to you and eat with you, and you with me" (Rev 3:20).

The Holy Trinity is in each one of you, more or less according to the room that you allow It, for, as you know, God never forces anyone. He asks and waits.

What do you feel drawn to do in response to these words?

August 19

Let mutual love continue. Do not neglect to show hospitality to strangers, for by doing that some have entertained angels without knowing it (Heb 13:1–2).

Ask Me to make My loving-kindness known to others through you. O don't lose a single opportunity of being the representative of God's goodness, even if it be only by a gesture.

What would being a representative of God's goodness look like in your life?

August 20

I slept, but my heart was awake.
Listen! my beloved is knocking.
"Open to me, my sister, my love,
   my dove, my perfect one" (Song 5:2).

Open the secret tabernacle of your heart to Me so
that we may speak together of our new love. The
words may be the same, but what an added weight
of love!

*Can you put into words what is stirring in
your heart when you hear "Open to me"?*

August 21

One thing I asked of the LORD,
    that will I seek after:
to live in the house of the LORD
    all the days of my life,
to behold the beauty of the LORD (Ps 27:4).

If you could only see My splendor in the tabernacle . . . My power and My tenderness and the guard of honor formed by My hosts of angels burning with zeal. What reverence, what a sense of nothingness you would feel! . . . You would see the utter unimportance of everything that is not love.

What image comes to mind when you think of the Lord's beauty?

August 22

When the wine gave out, the mother of Jesus said to him, "They have no wine" (Jn 2:3).

Give yourself to Mary so that you may walk in her ways. She is ready to help you because she knows God and His desires, and she knows you in your difficulties, almost all of which come from human pride. So give yourselves often from the depths of your heart. You must admit that with such a Father, mother, and brother you are greatly helped along life's way.

Have you considered that Mary knows you and is ready to help you?

August 23

[May you be] strengthened with every power, in accord with his glorious might, for all endurance and patience, with joy, giving thanks to the Father (Col 1:11–12).

You know what that is—just a fly. You brush it away once, several times; in the end it always goes away. Your little spiritual trials are your devotions. Be patient and cheerful.

Make the decision right now that you will not let your distracting thoughts or imaginings bother you in this time with Jesus.

August 24

"Come," my heart says, "seek his face!"
    Your face, LORD, do I seek. . . .
Wait for the LORD;
    be strong, and let your heart take courage;
    wait for the LORD! (Ps 27:8, 14).

Take courage, since I am helping you, and kindle your desires. Desires are prayers. They are swift arrows. Take aim and may the mark be struck with power.

What kind of desires do you feel Jesus is hoping for from you? Ask Him for the courage you need.

August 25

You have ravished my heart, my sister, my
bride,
  you have ravished my heart with a glance of
  your eyes (Song 4:9).

Don't you know that because of My compassion a single act of perfect love atones for a whole life-time? That one humble and tender look from you pierces My heart with love? That I am sensitive to every cry of your hearts?

Imagine a God who loves this much! How do you feel called to respond?

August 26

I do not occupy myself with things
  too great and too marvelous for me.
But I have calmed and quieted my soul,
  like a weaned child with its mother
    (Ps 131:1–2).

When I ask you to be simple, I mean above all in your relations with Me. Don't get the idea that I need any special words or gestures; just be yourself. Who is closer to you than God?

What would being yourself with Jesus look like for you? Talk with Him about it.

August 27

Love your enemies and pray for those who per-
secute you, so that you may be children of your
Father in heaven (Mt 5:44f.).

In the world at this very moment there are beloved
children of Mine who want to be total strangers to
Me. Pray for them in their terrible poverty. Pray
with the riches that you have received expressly to
help others.

*Right now, pray for the spiritually destitute,
those you know and those unknown to you.*

August 28

The sacrifice acceptable to God is a broken
   spirit;
   a broken and contrite heart, O God, you
      will not despise (Ps 51:17).

My heart has seen everything and is ready to forget because it listens to your words of distress and
humility. Oh, the power of repentance! The sacrifice that pleases Me is a cleft and contrite heart.
Such a heart I do not despise.

*Can you see a way forward in repentance?
Jesus is calling you, ready to forget the mistakes
of the past.*

August 29

"For truly I tell you, whoever gives you a cup of water to drink because you bear the name of Christ will by no means lose the reward" (Mk 9:41).

You forget what you do for Me and what you say to Me; you leave it in the past. But all these things are eternally present for Me, and you will find them again one day exactly as you gave them to Me.

When you realize that Jesus holds all your gifts as precious, what stirs in your heart?

August 30

"The bread of God is that which comes down from heaven and gives life to the world" (Jn 6:33).

Here is a way of doing everything well: act as though you had just left the Communion table, and you will see how your interior life blossoms out in peaceful communion with your heart.

Imagine how it would be if you always acted as though Jesus had just come to you in Holy Communion.

August 31

This is the boldness we have in him, that if we ask anything according to his will, he hears us. And if we know that he hears us in whatever we ask, we know that we have obtained the requests made of him (1 Jn 5:14–15).

Ask Me for every grace. Don't ever think, "That's impossible. He couldn't give me that."

Can you grasp Jesus' powerful desire to be asked? Resolve to ask Him for something you need, even if it is seemingly impossible.

SEPTEMBER

September 1

When I thought, "My foot is slipping,"
   your steadfast love, O LORD, held me up
      (Ps 94:18).

As you look back over your life, don't you see that My will was always for your good? This is because I love you and it's the same for everyone, since I love each of you individually. I see you all differently; I see every detail about you, you understand? My love is not a global love.

How do you desire to respond to Jesus' individual, unique love for you?

September 2

Love is patient, love is kind. It is not jealous, [love] is not pompous, it is not inflated, it is not rude, it does not seek its own interests, it is not quick-tempered, it does not brood over injury, it does not rejoice over wrongdoing but rejoices with the truth (1 Cor 13:4–6).

The more Christian one is—that is, the more one is Mine—the kinder one is. So you be the kindest of all women.

What would being the "kindest of all women" look like for you? How do you feel drawn to respond to this invitation?

September 3

The mountains may depart
   and the hills be removed,
but my steadfast love shall not depart from
      you,
   and my covenant of peace shall not be
      removed,
says the LORD, who has compassion on you
   (Isa 54:10).

I'm loving you even when you are not thinking of loving Me, and I'm preparing blessings you never think to ask for. A look, a gesture for Me, and I give you everything, little child of My heart.

Ask Jesus about the blessings He has prepared for you that you have not yet asked for.

September 4

Lord, you know everything; you know that I love you (Jn 21:17).

Begin afresh every day as though it were the very first. You are forever at the beginning. Don't be afraid, for I am with you, and I know. Is there anything I don't know? All the same, I like you to tell Me where you have failed and to explain yourself to Me. It brings out your confidence in Me.

Wouldn't you like to try beginning every day afresh?

September 5

God chose the foolish of the world to shame the wise, and God chose the weak of the world to shame the strong, and God chose the lowly and despised of the world, those who count for nothing, to reduce to nothing those who are something, so that no human being might boast before God (1 Cor 1:27–29).

Who is pure? There are only sinners or those who have been purified. Woe to people who pride themselves on not yielding to a temptation that never bothered them.

Talk to Jesus about the recognition that everyone is a sinner. Consider that true humility is a relief from the expectation of perfection.

September 6

Commit your way to the LORD;
   trust in him, and he will act (Ps 37:5).

Even if you don't see the result of your prayers or efforts, don't let this hold you back. Just keep in mind that I know everything, and place yourself once more in the hands of your Redeemer.

When Jesus says you won't know the results of your efforts, how do you feel drawn to respond?

September 7

The prayer of the humble pierces the clouds,
    and it will not rest until it reaches its goal;
it will not desist until the Most High responds
    (Sir 35:21).

One who understands My desire opens his heart at all times. I have so much love for a soul that its faintest call finds an echo in Me. Don't be afraid of expressing yourself. Put your mouth to My ear. I'm listening.

What do you want to whisper to Him? Don't be afraid.

September 8

She gave birth to her firstborn son and wrapped him in bands of cloth, and laid him in a manger, because there was no place for them in the inn (Lk 2:7).

The saints thought only of Me all their lives. Accept the help of My mother for this, and think of Me with all the tenderness of which you are able. Tenderness honors Me more than reverence. It consoles Me. I was going to say it pays Me.

Ask Mary to show you how to console Jesus with your tenderness.

September 9

By this everyone will know that you are my disciples, if you have love for one another (Jn 13:35).

Never miss a chance to be kind, and give pleasure as though it were I who gave and not you. A thoughtful gesture can do so much good. It can be the beginning of a miracle. It takes only a little kindness to melt a heart, you know.

In what way could you allow His kindness and thoughtfulness to flow through you?

September 10

I will do whatever you ask in my name, so that the Father may be glorified in the Son. If in my name you ask me for anything, I will do it (Jn 14:13–14).

I am here with treasures. If you don't ask Me for them, how can I give them to you? If you didn't tell Me often that you love Me, where would be My joy?

Imagine what treasures Jesus wants to give you. What stirs in your heart?

September 11

"Which one of you, having a hundred sheep and losing one of them, does not leave the ninety-nine in the wilderness and go after the one that is lost until he finds it? When he has found it, he lays it on his shoulders and rejoices" (Lk 15:4–5).

Pray for those who are afraid. How can they be? How could anyone be afraid of such a good Shepherd? Even the very little lambs climb on His knees and rest there. And this is the Shepherd's joy.

Do you know people who are afraid of God or afraid of life? Pray for them.

September 12

How lovely is your dwelling place,
    O Lord of hosts!
My soul longs, indeed it faints
    for the courts of the Lord;
my heart and my flesh sing for joy
    to the living God (Ps 84:1–2).

You know how cold and sad an empty house is, how different from one that's filled with youth and life and joy. That is the difference between a soul where I cannot live because sin has driven Me out and the soul that I in-dwell. Say to yourself often, "He is in me."

Sit quietly and consider what it means to have Jesus dwelling in you.

September 13

So be imitators of God, as beloved children, and live in love, as Christ loved us and handed himself over for us as a sacrificial offering to God for a fragrant aroma (Eph 5:1–2).

Offer Me everything. Absolutely everything, united to My life on earth. What wealth! Give it to poor sinners, most of them are just ignorant. You have known and received so much. Take pains to help them.

Gratefully marvel at all you have received. What are you called to share?

September 14

Now those who belong to Christ [Jesus] have crucified their flesh with its passions and desires (Gal 5:24).

Be crucified with Me. To be crucified is to be stretched against your desires, against the love of self . . . in poverty, obscurity, and obedience to the Father. Remember that the crucifixion is the prelude to the resurrection, that is, to all joys.

What would being stretched against your desires look like for you? How do you want to respond to Jesus?

September 15

Blessed are you among women, and blessed is the fruit of your womb (Lk 1:41–42).

Why don't you offer everything by the hands of your mother, by her sorrowful and immaculate heart . . . ? You know that she loves those two titles because I gave her first her very pure conception, then suffering for the greater part of her life. And everything that God gave her she received so very humbly with love and respect.

Ask Mary for help in accepting everything as she did.

September 16

"Take my yoke upon you, and learn from me; for I am gentle and humble in heart, and you will find rest for your souls" (Mt 11:29).

You must go out of the door of yourself to enter into Me. And if you do this humbly and joyously, what joy you give Me! I forget the suffering that so many cause Me and I take refuge with all My favors in your heart-center.

Have you considered that your openness with Jesus can bring Him joy? Speak to Him about this.

September 17

But truly God has listened;
> he has given heed to the words of my prayer
> > (Ps 66:19).

Is it so difficult to talk with Me? Everything that interests you, every little detail of your life, tell me about it. I'll listen with such attention and joy. If you only knew.

Talk to Him about whatever is on your mind at this moment, knowing that He is listening attentively.

September 18

But God proves his love for us in that while we were still sinners Christ died for us (Rom 5:8).

My love is the source of everything. Did you think it was My pity? My pity, yes, but moved by this love of Mine that is greater than all other loves. I can only teach you about it little by little, because you are so fragile.

Ask Him to teach you a little about His love today.

September 19

[And] be kind to one another, compassionate, forgiving one another as God has forgiven you in Christ (Eph 4:32).

If I have fulfilled you, it is for the sake of others too. Be ready to pass on to them with love all that you have received. You owe Me this; you also owe it to them. Believe with all your heart that in sharing this overflow of graces you will help many others.

Remember and reflect on so many ways you have received from God.

September 20

I even consider everything as a loss because of the supreme good of knowing Christ Jesus my Lord. For his sake I have accepted the loss of all things and I consider them so much rubbish, that I may gain Christ and be found in him (Phil 3:8–9).

Don't drag your past along with you constantly if it burdens you and hinders you from coming close to Me. Just as you are, throw yourself into My arms for your joy.

What a relief to consider that you do not need to keep carrying past baggage. Decide now to let it go and entrust yourself to Jesus.

September 21

Whoever wishes to be great among you must be your servant, and whoever wishes to be first among you must be your slave; just as the Son of Man came not to be served but to serve, and to give his life a ransom for many (Mt 20:26–28).

We'll walk together, patiently striving day by day. My very little one, understand Me: it's the patient daily efforts that give value to small things.

What change of perspective is Jesus calling you to? Tell Him you want to walk with Him today.

September 22

What will separate us from the love of Christ? Will anguish, or distress, or persecution, or famine, or nakedness, or peril, or the sword? . . . No, in all these things we conquer overwhelmingly through him who loved us (Rom 8:35, 37).

Have this blessed assurance that the anxieties and toil of the world are not to be compared with the reward. And the reward is your Christ. Just think of it!

Imagine what it would be like to have the perspective that your current anxieties and struggle are nothing compared to the joy of heaven.

September 23

Give ear, O LORD, to my prayer;
  listen to my cry of supplication.
In the day of my trouble I call on you,
  for you will anwer me (Ps 86:6–7).

Each person has his own way of asking. Let yours be warm and long, joyous as though you already had the answer, loving because you are sure that you are loved, generous as always, and charming, since you are full of My gifts.

Has it occurred to you that your way of making requests could be charming to Him?

September 24

Hannah prayed and said,
"My heart exults in the LORD;
    my strength is exalted in my God"
    (1 Sam 2:1).

But My close friends, why, why don't they call louder to Me from their heart's depths? If only their belief were less like unbelief! If their hope were fixed upon My help . . . And if, in all simplicity, their love loved Me more.

When you hear Jesus' personal plea, what stirs in your own heart? Ask Him loudly for the graces you need.

September 25

Trust in him, and he will help you;
    make your ways straight, and hope in him
      (Sir 2:6).

Have you noticed how people talk among themselves, discussing all their personal affairs? They spend so much time this way and it does them so little good. Don't you think that if they gave themselves to Me, their friend, I should rejoice to have My place in their thoughts and I should know how to reward their confidence?

Talk to Jesus, confide in Him, and ask Him for any advice you need.

September 26

Truly I tell you, just as you did it to one of the least of these who are members of my family, you did it to me (Mt 25:40).

How ready you would be to smile at everyone if you could only see your Jesus in them. So remember this and don't economize your kindness.

What would seeing Jesus in everyone look like in your life? Talk to Jesus about it.

September 27

Who is wise and understanding among you? Show by your good life that your works are done with gentleness born of wisdom (Jas 3:13).

Each soul is the object of My special love. That is why I am so grateful to those who are resourceful in bringing back sinners to Me. Keep this in mind, then. I gave My life for them in the most atrocious torture . . . So speak gently to them. Speak with tenderness. A brusque remark could drive them farther away.

Express to Jesus what comes into your mind and heart at these words.

September 28

Your words were found, and I ate them,
    and your words became to me a joy
    and the delight of my heart;
for I am called by your name,
    O LORD, God of hosts (Jer 15:16).

Enjoy Me. Give yourself a rest from saying prayers so that you may enjoy My love.

What would it look like right now for you to rest in Jesus' love? Decide that today you will enjoy Him!

September 29

Those who eat my flesh and drink my blood have eternal life, and I will raise them up on the last day (Jn 6:54).

My child, even the angels envy this beautiful life of ours—this oneness. Oh, this intimacy in time that leads straight to eternity . . . this heartwarming way of consoling your God! Since you love Him, could you ever fail to make every effort to cultivate this life with Him by the help of His grace?

Marvel at the amazing gift of closeness to Him that He is offering you.

September 30

How sweet are your words to my taste,
    sweeter than honey to my mouth! ...
Your word is a lamp to my feet
    and a light to my path (Ps 119:103, 105).

Take My gospels and keep them always with you.
You will please Me by doing this.

*Express your thanks to Jesus for the gift of the
four Gospels, through which we learn about
His life. Resolve now to read them often.*

OCTOBER

October 1

I am the vine, you are the branches. Those who abide in me and I in them bear much fruit, because apart from me you can do nothing (Jn 15:5).

When you were little you wanted someone to take your hand when you crossed the street. Ask Me often to take your hand, because you are always little. Don't ever think that you can do anything good without Me.

What would having this childlike trust in Jesus look like in your life?

October 2

"There is joy in the presence of the angels of God over one sinner who repents" (Lk 15:10).

Just imagine what it would be like if at this moment all the people on the earth let Me live in them by grace. What a spectacle for heaven! Because you are all performing before the angels and saints.

Look at the day ahead, conscious that you are always living in the presence of your guardian angel. Decide to act with this awareness today.

October 3

The angel said to her, "The Holy Spirit will come upon you, and the power of the Most High will overshadow you; therefore the child to be born will be holy; he will be called Son of God (Lk 1:35).

Honor My mother in the Father's eternal thought because her life was the perfect unfoldment of the divine pattern for her.

Look to Mary for an example of fulfilling God's will and ask Jesus to accomplish his plan in you today.

October 4

But may I never boast except in the cross of our Lord Jesus Christ, through which the world has been crucified to me, and I to the world (Gal 6:14).

Quicken your faith and confidence. Speak to My extravagance of love and long to respond with your own. Think of Saint Francis of Assisi, the saintly missionaries and martyrs. Didn't they seem ridiculous in the eyes of the world? They were so engulfed in the love of their Savior that all things seemed as nothing to them. So don't be afraid.

Are you afraid of seeming ridiculous to others? Talk to Him about it.

October 5

The prayer of the humble pierces the clouds,
    and it will not rest until it reaches its goal;
it will not desist until the Most High responds
    (Sir 35:21).

Like a poor man I'm waiting at your door for what you want to give Me. Try to find the moment when you pleased Me the most today. Wasn't it when you were little with the little ones—with the greatest simplicity?

*What moment of the past day do you think
was the most pleasing to Him?*

October 6

And remember, I am with you always, to the end of the age (Mt 28:20).

Never alone; you know that. Then let it be a source of strength to you. Strength to speak to Me, since I am there. Strength to act, since I can help you, particularly when you speak to others. Ask Me to speak through you.

What stirs in your heart at the thought that Jesus is always with you?

October 7

On entering the house, they saw the child with Mary his mother; and they knelt down and paid him homage (Mt 2:11).

All the month of the Rosary, call My mother "Our Lady of Love" and say, "Our Lady of Love, give me love." How can you make progress all by yourself? Let yourself be carried in stronger arms, just as you did when you were little. Don't be ashamed of being weak and imperfect.

Ask Our Lady of Love to help you make progress in loving today.

October 8

Know that I am with you and will keep you wherever you go . . . ; for I will not leave you until I have done what I have promised you (Gen 28:15).

My child, ponder more often on the value of the present moment, the danger of going back over the past and the uselessness of gazing into the future. Just live the little moment that you hold in your hands. Simply and lovingly.

What would living in the present moment look like for you?

October 9

"What eye has not seen, and ear has not heard,
and what has not entered the human heart,
what God has prepared for those who love
him" (1 Cor 2:9).

Don't be alarmed when your imagination gallops.
It is your will that concerns Me. I died to make
your will Mine. Do you want to give it all to Me?
Don't just treat Me as the guest of your great
moments, but as the beloved you never leave. You
know what "never" means?

*Tell Him you want to be all His—mind, will,
and heart—always.*

October 10

You prepare a table before me
in the presence of my enemies;
you anoint my head with oil;
my cup overflows (Ps 23:5).

And while you are talking to Me, I'll continue to heap blessings upon you, for My heart is filled with them, and to give eases it of its burden. It takes a mere nothing from you to make it overflow.

Have you considered that Jesus has so much to give that it is a relief for Him to lavish it on you?

October 11

The LORD is faithful in all his words,
and gracious in all his deeds.
The LORD upholds all who are falling,
and raises up all who are bowed down
(Ps 145:13–14).

Remember that I want your perfection more than you do. Do you ask Me for this every day? Those who are thirsty never stop asking for a drink. Are you saddened by your usual mediocrity? If you weren't, how could I help you? Your cry, full of hope, would be music to Me. So learn, learn to cry to Me.

Talk to Jesus about your desire, and His desire, for your holiness.

October 12

Yet it was you who took me from the womb;
you kept me safe on my mother's breast.
On you I was cast from my birth,
and since my mother bore me you have
been my God (Ps 22: 9–10).

Mother . . . not only Mine but yours. Throughout this whole day, call her your mother.

Jesus wants to share His mother with you. Tell her what is in your heart and on your mind right now.

October 13

But grace was given to each of us according to the measure of Christ's gift . . . for building up the body of Christ (Eph 4:7, 12).

It is I who gave you everything—your heart, your understanding, your memory. It is I who gave you an imagination capable of stirring your heart. Is it too much to expect that you will use My gifts for Me?

Reflect on these gifts you have been given. How can you respond to Jesus' hopeful expectation?

October 14

Simeon blessed them and said to his mother Mary, "This child is destined for the falling and the rising of many in Israel, and to be a sign that will be opposed so that the inner thoughts of many will be revealed—and a sword will pierce your own soul too" (Lk 2:34–35).

Never leave your immaculate mother. She won't leave you either. She loves you even more than your own dear mother. She suffered more to give birth to you, for she bore My death. Queen of Martyrs! If suffering increases love, just imagine the tenderness she feels for you.

Have you considered the tenderness Mary has for you?

October 15

The LORD is my strength and my shield;
    in him my heart trusts;
so I am helped, and my heart exults,
    and with my song I give thanks to him
        (Ps 28:7).

Always trust. Trust more and more—even to the point of expecting a miracle. Don't stop half way or you will set limits to My love. When you have unfolded your confidence you will unfold it still more without ever being able to exceed what I expect of you.

What would having this kind of trust look like for you?

October 16

We have known and believe the love that God has for us. God is love, and those who abide in love abide in God, and God abides in them (1 Jn 4:16).

Isn't it perfectly clear to you now that My love arranged all this for you? Then why didn't this thought occur to you without My having to remind you? You always think that these things just happen. Nothing just happens. I am in everything. And I am all love.

Can you see how His love has arranged things for you lately?

October 17

What you sow is not brought to life unless it dies (1 Cor 15:36).

To offer a sacrifice doesn't mean that you won't feel the pain of it; on the contrary, the pain will return many times to stir up its bitter waters. But at each new tide of distress, come back again to Me in a spirit of sacrifice, and a rainbow of blessings will light up the earth.

Is Jesus inviting you to offer or renew a particular sacrifice in your life?

October 18

"The greatest among you must become like the youngest, and the leader like one who serves" (Lk 22:26).

This is the sign by which I know those who belong to Me: they leave behind even their own desires to follow Me. These give Me to others unawares, for the Spirit possesses them and expresses Himself through them.

What stirs in your heart when you read these words? Talk to Jesus about it.

October 19

Now to him who is able to accomplish far more than all we ask or imagine, by the power at work within us, to him be glory in the church and in Christ Jesus (Eph 3:20–21).

You can do so much for God's glory in the time left to you before eternity. Offer yourself often to Him as a docile instrument. Tell Him you want His will to be done in you. Tell Him of your impatience for His kingdom to come.

Pray the Our Father slowly, truly asking that God's kingdom come.

October 20

The LORD said to him, "I have heard your prayer and your plea, which you made before me; I have consecrated this house that you have built, and put my name there forever; my eyes and my heart will be there for all time" (1 Kings 9:3).

When you are in church, get rid of all thoughts and cares of the day. Just put them aside as you take off a garment. And be all Mine.

Consider that Jesus wants you to be all His. What would it look like for you to be able to do this in your life?

October 21

Blessed are those who are invited to the marriage supper of the Lamb (Rev 19:9).

Sometimes you envy the people who lived in My day. And yet, apart from the apostles, they didn't have Communion as frequently as you; they didn't have My Eucharist every morning in the depths of their hearts.

Express your gratitude for the Eucharist and all the spiritual gifts that you have access to.

October 22

Those who love me will keep my word, and my Father will love them, and we will come to them and make our home with them (Jn 14:23–24).

Don't worry if you don't hear My voice. Don't begin to think I am far from you. I'm in the very center of your being with the Father and the Holy Spirit. Give yourself to Us.

How is Jesus calling you to remember His constant presence and desire for you?

October 23

Our Father in heaven,
    hallowed be your name.
    Your kingdom come.
    Your will be done, on earth as it is in
        heaven (Mt 6:9–10).

My will is all love. It is out of love that you ask Me for it, and when the sum of all the love on earth is greater than the sum of hate, that will be a step forward. Hate is not from heaven. Hate is the very breath of hell.

Pray this line of the Lord's Prayer: "Thy will be done," and know that you are praying for the love of heaven to be also on earth.

October 24

"He said to me, 'You are my servant,
Israel, in whom I will be glorified'"
(Isa 49:3).

You are only an instrument. But be that; be always
ready to serve Me. Serve Me, not yourself. You're
dependent on Me. I'm your Employer. Thank Me
for wishing to make use of you. Aren't you happy
with your employer? Could you ever say that I
don't look after you?

*Reflect on your complete dependence on God.
What moves in your heart?*

October 25

I sought the LORD, and he answered me,
and delivered me from all my fears.
Look to him, and be radiant;
so your faces shall never be ashamed
(Ps 34:4–5).

And are you ever so busy that you haven't even a moment to glance at Me? It would enrich Me, for I am poor when it comes to the thoughts of My children. So very poor—I who never leave you.

Decide to "enrich" Jesus by thinking of Him more often today. What could be a reminder for you?

October 26

Set me as a seal upon your heart,
  as a seal upon your arm;
for love is strong as death,
  passion fierce as the grave.
Its flashes are flashes of fire,
  a raging flame.
Many waters cannot quench love,
  neither can floods drown it (Song 8:6–7).

Seize upon every opportunity to be one with Me. If you only knew what a joy this union with souls on earth is to Me, you would understand that I reward those who offer Me the frequent thoughts of their hearts.

Have you considered that you can bring Him so much joy?

October 27

She opens her hand to the poor,
    and reaches out her hands to the needy. . . .
Strength and dignity are her clothing
    (Prov 31:20, 25).

Acquire the delicate art of letting your neighbor feel that you stretch out the arms of your heart to him. Should this be so difficult if we think of God in him?

What would it look like for you to practice this "delicate art"?

October 28

When you send forth your spirit, they are
created;
and you renew the face of the ground.
May the glory of the LORD endure forever;
may the LORD rejoice in his works
(Ps 104:30–31).

If you surrender and let the Spirit flow in, you give
joy to the saints in heaven and glory to the Father
because you have begun to understand His love.
Oh, My child, give the Father the best of yourself.

*What image comes to mind when you envi-
sion opening your heart and giving the Spirit
permission to flow in and work in you?*

October 29

"I have said this to you, so that in me you may have peace. In the world you face persecution. But take courage; I have conquered the world!" (Jn 16:33)

If you suffer, suffer with Me. All these discomforts caused by the weather—I bore them all, like you, on the open roads. Always be one with Me in everything that happens to you.

How do you feel called to respond to this invitation to oneness with Jesus?

October 30

You do well if you really fulfill the royal law according to the scripture, "You shall love your neighbor as yourself" (Jas 2:8).

Reach up closer and closer to your Maker. He created you. He knows all about you and how best you can serve Him. And what your share is in the sanctification of the world; for each one of you has some special contribution to make. What sorrow for you if you were to fail! If you didn't respond to the call!

What stirs in your heart at the thought of God's plan for you?

October 31

For we know that if our earthly dwelling, a tent, should be destroyed, we have a building from God, a dwelling not made with hands, eternal in heaven. For in this tent we groan, longing to be further clothed with our heavenly habitation (2 Cor 5:1–2).

Keep this thought always before you: it is when you are living on earth that I enjoy you, My beloved faithful ones. But in heaven it will be you who will enjoy Me.

Have you considered that you give Him enjoyment? Tell Him you are looking forward to being with Him in heaven.

NOVEMBER

November 1

I consider that the sufferings of this present time are as nothing compared with the glory to be revealed for us (Rom 8:18).

Hooow fleeting and small the earthly sacrifices are! Do you know that the saints in heaven would envy you: their time of sacrifice is over. Don't lose any time, since you told Me that everything was for Me.

Have you considered that you have opportunities that the saints no longer have? Ask their help to truly see the value of time.

November 2

I tell you, her sins, which were many, have been forgiven; hence she has shown great love. But the one to whom little is forgiven, loves little (Lk 7:47).

Take your soul in your hands and look at your day. Weigh up the love you have given Me during the hours that have gone by. And remember: you will be judged according to the measure of your love.

What would it look like for you to measure your day by the love given instead of by how much was accomplished?

November 3

But our citizenship is in heaven (Phil 3:20).

You will see life, your neighbor, service for God's glory from a new viewpoint that will completely change your usual petty opinions. The saints saw things differently from others and that is why they seemed to lead strange lives. They didn't have the same eyes.

Ask Jesus for the eyes to see your life from His point of view today.

November 4

The kingdom of heaven is like treasure hidden in a field, which someone found and hid; then in his joy he goes and sells all that he has and buys that field (Mt 13:44).

You must long for heaven, because this is the same as to long for Me and it glorifies Me. Even when you have such a distorted picture of Me, yearn for Me, for this is a triple act of faith, hope and love.

What draws you when you think of heaven?
How do you envision it?

November 5

Jesus said to Simon Peter, "Simon son of John, do you love me more than these?" He said to him, "Yes, Lord; you know that I love you." Jesus said to him, "Feed my lambs" (Jn 21:15).

Love Me in all kinds of ways. Love to make amends, to comfort Me, to thank Me, to glorify Me, to obtain, to please Me, and then love just for the sake of loving. That's what the saints in heaven are doing and would you believe it, it is forever the story of My passion that is perpetually renewed.

Decide how you will love Him today.

November 6

I will rejoice in the LORD;
  I will exult in the God of my salvation.
GOD, the Lord, is my strength;
  he makes my feet like the feet of a deer,
  and makes me tread upon the heights
    (Hab 3:18–19).

What could ever harm you? You are God's child and Christ is your brother. Isn't that a wellspring of joy? Escape from yourself. Forget all earthly cares.

How do you feel called to respond to these words of Jesus? Talk to Him about your earthly cares.

November 7

To the one who pleases him God gives wisdom and knowledge and joy (Eccl 2:26).

Just keep your will for Me; that's enough. Your will in Mine—that's everything—for My joy and yours. I want you to be completely joyous. You will be when you have emptied yourself of self. Then you will no longer feel the gravity of life, but the gentle and buoyant breath of uplifting joy.

What could this joy of self-emptying look like for you?

November 8

And the ransomed of the LORD shall return,
 and come to Zion with singing;
everlasting joy shall be upon their heads;
 they shall obtain joy and gladness,
 and sorrow and sighing shall flee away
 (Isa 35:10).

Give this joy to your Lord God, little child of His. Tell Me all about your desire for Me and I'll make it grow. Even if you don't desire Me, tell Me so I'll give you the desire. And I'll make it increase to the point where you will long to leave the earth to meet Me.

What stirs in your heart at the thought of desire for God?

November 9

Then Jesus said to them, "Very truly, I tell you, it was not Moses who gave you the bread from heaven, but it is my Father who gives you the true bread from heaven" (Jn 6:32).

How often I have had abundant treasures in My tabernacle all ready to give, but no one came to ask Me for them.

Ask Jesus for all the treasures He wants to give you, and then thank Him even before you receive anything.

November 10

Let love be sincere; hate what is evil, hold on to what is good; love one another with mutual affection; anticipate one another in showing honor (Rom 12:9–10).

You often feel sorry that you were not alive when I was on earth so that you could have been with Me. Be fully aware of Me in those around you, and, without stopping to contemplate Me, serve Me in them. Later on you will be glad of this.

Right now, decide to serve Jesus in those around you today.

November 11

Do not neglect to do good and to share what you have, for such sacrifices are pleasing to God (Heb 13:16).

If I give you favors of tenderness, it is to encourage you to stoop to make sacrifices for your brothers. Give as you have received. I want to go down to the very heart of your heart and make My home there.

What would it be like for you to welcome Jesus into the depths of your heart?

November 12

I do not call you servants any longer, because the servant does not know what the master is doing; but I have called you friends, because I have made known to you everything that I have heard from my Father (Jn 15:15).

Why should you use long sentences and difficult words to speak to Me? Just talk with the utmost simplicity as you do with your family and intimate friends. I belong to the inner circle don't I?

Imagine talking to Jesus just as to your family and friends. What moves in your heart?

November 13

From now on the crown of righteousness awaits me, which the Lord, the just judge, will award to me on that day, and not only to me, but to all who have longed for his appearance (2 Tim 4:8).

Heaven is not far from the earth when you ask it to come. Live more with the saints. They can all help you to love Me more, now that they know. Oh, this science of love!

Everyone who is in heaven is a saint—not just those officially so named. Pick a saint to talk to and go to them for help in the day ahead.

November 14

May the Lord direct your hearts to the love of God (2 Thes 3:5).

You make amends for yourself and you make amends for the ingratitude of so many others. Do they think of Me with a little affection even once a year? Do they accept the thought of My love for each one of them? When will they realize that time—the span of earthly life—is too short, that I need all eternity to love them?

Express to Jesus whatever moves you in these words.

November 15

Blessed are those who trust in the LORD,
  whose trust is the LORD.
They shall be like a tree planted by water,
  sending out its roots by the stream.
It shall not fear when heat comes,
  and its leaves shall stay green (Jer 17:7–8).

You can't compute holiness like a column of figures. A single act of love with absolute abandonment and trust can make a saint even at the moment of death. And how this honors Me!

Right now, pray for whoever is at the moment of death and has not turned to God with trust.

November 16

For God alone my soul waits in silence,
  for my hope is from him.
He alone is my rock and my salvation,
  my fortress; I shall not be shaken
    (Ps 62:5–6).

Seize upon every opportunity of keeping silent and give Me this silence just as though you were picking a flower for Me. Oh, this beautiful silence full of peace, humility, serenity, and intimacy with God! How much you can obtain in these blessed moments!

Have you considered intentionally making silence part of your day?

November 17

Very truly, I tell you, unless a grain of wheat falls into the earth and dies, it remains just a single grain; but if it dies, it bears much fruit (Jn 12:24).

One little lonely soul, lost among the people of the earth but united to the Son of God in the fullness of His blessed will may, through His compassionate heart, become an instrument for the uplifting of others.

When you realize the effect you can have on history through your union with Him, what stirs in your heart?

November 18

How precious is your steadfast love, O God!
(Ps 36:7)

Look at Me often. When one is in love, what
sweetness there is in a look! As for Me, I keep you
always before My face. Tell Me that you long to
give Me the same love-token. Oh, I realize you're
carried away by a hundred and one things in life.
But make it your first concern to be with Me.

*How can you make Jesus your first concern
today?*

November 19

For by grace you have been saved through faith, and this is not from you; it is the gift of God; it is not from works, so no one may boast (Eph 2:8–9).

If you have the intention of loving Me when you pray, I'll accept your prayer even when you are distracted.

Renew this intention of love in your prayer right now, and decide not to worry about distractions today.

November 20

"Do not work for the food that perishes, but for the food that endures for eternal life, which the Son of Man will give you" (Jn 6:27).

Don't you live as though you were all going to remain on earth forever? You so seldom give even a furtive glance at the life beyond, at your residence of tomorrow, when your heart should already be there, thanking Me, praising Me, adoring Me every day and in every action of the day.

What is Jesus inviting you to in these words?

November 21

"I will put enmity between you and the
woman,
    and between your offspring and hers;
he will strike your head,
    and you will strike his heel" (Gen 3:15).

[My mother] will help you on your uphill climb;
it is strenuous work climbing the mountain of perfection . . . The other Eve was called the first
woman, but My mother is the woman who crushed
the head of the serpent.

Have you considered how powerful Mary is?
Ask her help today in whatever difficulties you
face.

November 22

For God will lead Israel with joy,
    in the light of his glory,
      with the mercy and righteousness that
        come from him (Bar 5:9).

Don't you grasp the fact that if you love Me and believe in My love, you surrender your whole self into My hands like a little child who doesn't even ask, "Where are you taking me?" but sets off joyously, hand in hand with his mother. How many blessings this happy confidence wins for you My children.

What would having this confidence look like for you?

November 23

Thus says the LORD,
    your Redeemer, the Holy One of Israel:
I am the LORD your God,
    who teaches you for your own good,
    who leads you in the way you should go
      (Isa 48:17).

You're not in error, only in the shadowland. Just feeling your way by faith. I planned it this way. So throw yourself into My arms. Say that you believe, that you hope, that you love, and commit your entire being to Me.

Express to Jesus what being "in the shadow-land" is like right now.

November 24

You will receive power when the Holy Spirit has come upon you; and you will be my witnesses . . . to the ends of the earth" (Acts 1:8).

[The Holy Spirit] makes the earth new and each one of you, too, according to your readiness to receive. He is infinite. Abandon yourself to Him. He is a consuming fire. Abandon yourself. He is the Comforter. Freed from self, ask Him to comfort through you.

How can you prepare to receive the fire and renewal of the Holy Spirit?

November 25

[L]ive in a manner worthy of the call you have received, with all humility and gentleness, with patience, bearing with one another through love, striving to preserve the unity of the spirit through the bond of peace (Eph 4:1–3).

My invitations are sent out at Baptism and again in My sacraments. It is for you to respond even though imperfectly. I am there, anxiously wondering what progress you will make from the cradle to the grave, ready to help you at your first cry. Don't ever get the idea that I'm far away.

When you realize how near Jesus is, what stirs within you?

November 26

My soul thirsts for God,
   for the living God.
When shall I come and behold
   the face of God? (Ps 42:2).

Offer Me [your] desire to see Me and Me only in everything. And I'll take it as a gift from you. Let nothing else count for you any more apart from what grieves or what pleases Me.

What would it look like for you to make daily choices based on what grieves or pleases Jesus?

November 27

For I am convinced that neither death, nor life, nor angels, nor principalities, nor present things, nor future things, nor powers, nor height, nor depth, nor any other creature will be able to separate us from the love of God in Christ Jesus our Lord (Rom 8:38–39).

Don't divide yourself into two—one part for you and the other for Me—since I long to have all of you and cherish this hope. Your love quenches My thirst.

Imagine what this total giving of self would be like. Ask Jesus for the ability to do it.

November 28

For in hope we were saved. Now hope that sees for itself is not hope. For who hopes for what one sees? But if we hope for what we do not see, we wait with endurance (Rom 8:24–25).

Oh, this great quality of hope! Practice it often so that it will grow in you. Don't you understand that the more you expect, the more you receive? Then expect even the impossible and you will have it.

How can you respond to this call of Jesus to make your hope wider and stronger?

November 29

I am coming soon; hold fast to what you have, so that no one may seize your crown (Rev 3:11).

Offer your death to Me now with complete detachment, ready even for heroism. Say, "Even if I didn't have to suffer death, I would choose it in order to be more one with Him." And in this way you will give Me the greatest glory a creature can give his Creator. Oh, precious death of the saints that echoes even in the heavenly courts of the Father's Home!

Show Jesus what is in your heart right now.

November 30

And just as Moses lifted up the serpent in the wilderness, so must the Son of Man be lifted up, that whoever believes in him may have eternal life. For God so loved the world that he gave his only Son, so that everyone who believes in him may not perish but may have eternal life (Jn 3:14–16).

Let us begin heaven. It would be such balm for Me. Do you want to give joy to your Savior-God? Then let your thoughts forever turn to Me.

Ask what Jesus means by "begin heaven." Imagine what it will be like to be with Him forever.

DECEMBER

December 1

I have loved you with an everlasting love (Jer 31:3).

Do you at last believe with all your heart that I created you in order to make you eternally happy? It was out of pure love that I made you—not for My own interest but for yours: to give you infinite bliss. O thank Me for your creation. . . . Never cease to look at My love enfolding you; and feeling loved, love Me.

Read this over and let it sink in—what a gift it was when God created you!

December 2

Let us rejoice and exult
    and give him the glory,
for the marriage of the Lamb has come,
    and his bride has made herself ready
        (Rev 19:7).

Why should My people offer Me only their trials? Don't you think your joys would please Me just as much—that is, if you give them with as much love: your smallest joys with your greatest love.

Recall some recent joys. Thank Jesus for them and offer them to Him with love.

December 3

My child, give me your heart,
    and let your eyes observe my ways
        (Prov 23:26).

So give me everything. Since we are one, could you be bold enough to say that there is something in your life that could not be for Me?

Reading this, does something specific come to mind that Jesus might want to talk with you about?

December 4

Love is patient, love is kind. It is not jealous, [love] is not pompous, it is not inflated, it is not rude, it does not seek its own interests, it is not quick-tempered, it does not brood over injury (1 Cor 13:4–5).

Every sin is a mockery of love, just as every virtue is the choice of love. And I am love. Try to understand the greatness of the principle. Get rid of your small self. Be My Self.

What would it look like for you to see every choice as related to love?

December 5

If you abide in me, and my words abide in you, ask for whatever you wish, and it will be done for you. My Father is glorified by this, that you bear much fruit and become my disciples (Jn 15:7–8).

Alone you can't do anything. But trusting in Me, leaning on Me, submerged in Me you can do everything. That's why I keep on saying, "Lose yourself in Me and humbly ask Me to act for you, and I'll act."

Lean on Jesus and ask Him to do everything in you and for you.

December 6

You anoint my head with oil;
     my cup overflows.
Surely goodness and mercy shall follow me
     all the days of my life (Ps 23:5–6).

Sometimes you like to prepare a lovely surprise and your whole heart is alight with the joy of it. Can you imagine My joy when you thank Me for making your cup run over? And I never come to the end of all My gifts.

Right now, express your gratitude for all that Jesus has delighted to prepare and give to you.

December 7

"Your heavenly Father knows that you need all these things. But strive first for the kingdom of God and his righteousness, and all these things will be given to you as well" (Mt 6:32–33).

Do everything with the same joy and love that you would have if you were in heaven. Seek nothing but My glory, and everything else will be given to you as well. Live wholly in the kingdom deep within you.

What would "living wholly in the kingdom" look like for you?

December 8

O daughter, you are blessed by the Most High God above all other women on earth; and blessed be the Lord God, who created the heavens and the earth (Jdt 13:18).

When you talk to My mother, be one with Me as I poured out My heart to her on the earth. Use your feet, your hands, and your breath as though they were Mine. What I want most is to be one with you.

Imagine Jesus with His mother, as a child and then as an adult. How is He calling you to imitate Him?

December 9

There is no fear in love, but perfect love casts out fear (1 Jn 4:18).

I don't want people to be afraid of Me anymore, but to see My heart full of love and to speak with Me as they would with a dearly beloved brother. For some I am unknown. For others, a stranger, a severe master, or an accuser. Few people come to Me as to one of a loved family. And yet My love is there, waiting for them.

When you consider these words, what stirs in your heart?

December 10

Let your adornment be the inner self with the lasting beauty of a gentle and quiet spirit, which is very precious in God's sight (1 Pet 3:4).

Follow My will alone so as to be sure of fulfilling it faithfully, even to the very smallest details. Fidelity places more value on small opportunities than on big ones. These are the little love-tokens, like the small coins that add up to a fortune.

Where do you feel drawn to grow in your fidelity?

December 11

Then the eyes of the blind shall be opened,
    and the ears of the deaf unstopped;
then the lame shall leap like a deer,
    and the tongue of the speechless sing for
      joy (Isa 35:5–6).

If only you had seen the joy of those I healed on the roads of Judea. They left Me singing praises to God. Sing every day in your heart and make Me known to others through joy. You want to make Me known, don't you?

Recall something Jesus has done for you and express your joy.

December 12

I determined to take her to live with me,
knowing that she would give me good counsel
and encouragement in cares and grief
    (Wis 8:9).

Ask My dear mother to help you respond to My
tenderness with your own. Alone you cannot, you
cannot, you cannot.

*What would it look like for you to respond to
Jesus with tenderness? Ask Mary's help.*

December 13

Those who drink of the water that I will give them will never be thirsty (Jn 4:14).

Don't you take a present when you are invited to a friend's home? And if your wealth were unlimited wouldn't your gifts be fabulous? Mine are like that. And as a friend who is fearful of burdening another with too great a sense of gratitude, I offer them so delicately that you take them for granted without always appreciating their value.

Resolve not to take Him for granted.

December 14

Yet I live, no longer I, but Christ lives in me; insofar as I now live in the flesh, I live by faith in the Son of God who has loved me and given himself up for me (Gal 2:20).

You are astonished by My love. There is only one explanation: God's extravagance. So just believe in all simplicity in this love of an all-powerful being, a being totally different from you. And give yourself up to His infinitely delicate and tender omnipotence.

How can you respond to Jesus' extravagant and infinite love?

December 15

I trusted in your steadfast love;
  my heart shall rejoice in your salvation
    (Ps 13:5).

Offer yourself to Me just as you are. Don't wait to be pleased with yourself. Be one with Me in your greatest shortcomings. I take them and restore you if you put your trust in Me. Have confidence. Who loves you the most?

Imagine what it would be like to go to Jesus just as you are, not waiting to be pleased with yourself.

December 16

The LORD delights in you (Isa 62:4).

Haven't you read that the more perfect and hidden an action the more excellent it is, because it is for Me alone? Did you know that there are deep forests, unfathomable oceans, and mountain peaks unknown to man where secret blossomings are for My extravagance of glory? So it is with the hidden life of a soul.

What do you feel drawn to do for Him alone?

December 17

My spirit rejoices in God my Savior (Lk 1:47).

Wherever you are, practice the presence of God.
It will help you to love Him, to have heart-to-heart
talks with Him. Since I am there, throw yourself
joyously into My arms. Oh, this joy of yours . . .
don't forget it; it enhances your love.

*Practice the presence of God right now—recall
with joy that you are in His presence.*

December 18

I think about all your deeds, I meditate on the
works of your hands.
I stretch out my hands to you;
my soul thirsts for you like a parched land
(Ps 143:5–6).

It's so easy for you to speak to Me, as to the matchless one in your heart. A glance, an inward smile . . .
Such simple things for you, and yet they mean so
much to Me.

*Have you considered the joy you can bring to
Jesus with just a glance or a smile?*

December 19

You are the God of the lowly, helper of the oppressed, upholder of the weak, protector of the forsaken, savior of those without hope (Jdt 9:11).

Since I am yours, you are rich. You are only poor when you count on yourselves and expect to act in your own unaided strength. How destitute you are then! But if you lay hold of My merits with humility and hope, what a priceless fortune is yours?

Thank Jesus for the lavish gift of Himself.

December 20

It is the LORD who goes before you. He will be with you; he will not fail you or forsake you. Do not fear or be dismayed (Deut 31:8).

It is with thoughts of our oneness that you will discover your duty to give happiness to those I have placed around you. Don't believe in chance, but learn to see the hand of your Father, your friend—the one who never leaves you—in everything that happens.

Decide now that you will look for God's hand in everything today.

December 21

"The LORD is my portion," says my soul,
"therefore I will hope in him" (Lam 3:24).

I am ready to give you everything you need if you ask Me. Why should you be afraid of asking when you have first of all praised and loved Me? I love everything about you, and it's the same for everyone. Aren't you all My children that I wanted to save?

With faith and trust, ask Him for anything and everything you need.

December 22

God created us for incorruption,
and made us in the image of his own eternity
(Wis 2:23).

In everything imitate your God. Ask Him to help
you to understand Him better. Until your soul
leaves your body you will not have seen God, but
you will have come to know Him better than by
sight, and from this knowledge will be born an
immense yearning to possess Him.

*Ask Jesus for understanding and knowledge of
God.*

December 23

He saves the humble (Job 22:29).

Even when you are doing the most ordinary things I am with you, because while I am the greatest, I am also the humblest, and nothing is ever deadly dull to Me. What is most obscure and despised only attracts Me more. So don't be afraid that I'll leave you at certain moments, for I love you all the time.

What moves in your heart at these words?

December 24

For God so loved the world that he gave his only Son, so that everyone who believes in him may not perish but may have eternal life (Jn 3:16).

In reality My secret and tender love is for every human being living in the world. There is not one who does not have a mysterious yearning for it. And how true it is that each one wants to see someone live My love so that he may discover the means of reaching Me.

Live His love today, for the sake of all those around you who do not know it.

December 25

They went with haste and found Mary and Joseph, and the child lying in the manger (Lk 2:16).

At Bethlehem do you think that Joseph could forget his two treasures for a single instant? His whole heart was centered on them. Be like him.

As you celebrate Christmas today, be like Saint Joseph—centered on God and on the happiness of those around you.

December 26

... [T]hough he was in the form of God,
    did not regard equality with God
    as something to be exploited,
but emptied himself,
    taking the form of a slave,
    being born in human likeness (Phil 2:5–7).

Sink down deep into the thought of My humility as a little child. I became humble for your sake. Would you like to come to the manger every day for lessons? ... I give you a rendezvous there. Call it a rendezvous of love.

What moves you when you look at the Child in the manger?

December 27

We know love by this, that he laid down his life for us—and we ought to lay down our lives for one another (1 Jn 3:16).

You know you must give great importance to the very little things of every passing moment because in My eyes, the eyes of God, only love will give value to what you do. I tell you this often because I don't want you to lose anything.

Decide to put love into everything you do today, and ask Him to help you see every opportunity.

December 28

[T]he fruit of the Spirit is love, joy, peace, patience, kindness, generosity, faithfulness, gentleness, self-control (Gal 5:22–23).

To be completely at peace, ask yourself at this close of the year: "Have I hurt someone?" This "someone" is My image. So go to that one, and speak as a sister. If his face displeases you, look at Mine through his.

Ask for the grace to do as He asks, then act.

December 29

For this momentary light affliction is producing for us an eternal weight of glory beyond all comparison, as we look not to what is seen but to what is unseen; for what is seen is transitory, but what is unseen is eternal (2 Cor 4:17–18).

Later on when you understand My love, you will be ready to return to earth for the sole purpose of yearning for Me even for a single instant. Ready to suffer, too, to the very end of time.

Imagine yearning for Jesus that much. Talk to Him about what stirs in your heart.

December 30

In all circumstances give thanks, for this is the will of God for you in Christ Jesus (1 Thes 5:18).

Always thank Me. I give you so much. If I were to give you a trial would you thank Me? You should. I do everything for the good of souls. Never doubt this, and believe in My love. Hope in My love.

Express your thanks to Jesus for the gifts of the past year.

December 31

[M]y heart's desire and prayer to God on their behalf is for salvation (Rom 10:1).

Dare as only love knows how to dare. Stay on My heart and be sure always to wake up there. Do this for the sake of all humanity, as though it were in your power to give Me every living person in a single instant. Learn to desire this. Desire is a beautiful fruit; you can quench My thirst with it. Go now and take Me with you.

Talk to Jesus about whatever in this passage most moved you.

Appendix

The words of Jesus for each day's devotion can be found in the book *He and I* on the following dates:

Devotional Date	*He and I* Selection	Devotional Date	*He and I* Selection
Jan 1	Sept 14, 1940	Jan 13	Sept 30, 1943
Jan 2	Jan 17, 1946	Jan 14	Nov 14, 1940
Jan 3	Feb 14, 1937	Jan 15	Sept 16, 1948
Jan 4	Dec 25, 1947	Jan 16	Sept 16, 1943
Jan 5	Oct 22, 1942	Jan 17	Feb 19, 1948
Jan 6	Aug 22, 1940	Jan 18	Oct 7, 1948
Jan 7	Nov 11, 1943	Jan 19	April 18, 20, 1937
Jan 8	Oct 15, 1943	Jan 20	July 29, 1943
Jan 9	April 7, 1940	Jan 21	Oct 24, 1940
Jan 10	Sept 21, 1940	Jan 22	Oct 15, 1943
Jan 11	July 25, 1946	Jan 23	Oct 17, 1946
Jan 12	March 29, 1940	Jan 24	May 27, 1948

Devotional Date	*He and I* Selection	Devotional Date	*He and I* Selection
Jan 25	Sept 12, 1946	Feb 17	Dec 1, 1949
Jan 26	Nov 6, 1940	Feb 18	Sept 21, 1940
Jan 27	Dec 22, 1948	Feb 19	Aug 18, 1942
Jan 28	May 3, 1945	Feb 20	June 15, 1937
Jan 29	March 30, 1937	Feb 21	March 18, 1948
Jan 30	Nov 11, 1940	Feb 22	Feb 2, 1950
Jan 31	Oct 7, 1943	Feb 23	Sept 30, 1943
Feb 1	Nov 19, 1942	Feb 24	May 9, 1946
Feb 2	July 29, 1943	Feb 25	Jan 13, 1949
Feb 3	April 30, 1937	Feb 26	Sept 24, 1942
Feb 4	April 1, 1948	Feb 27	Nov 11, 1948
Feb 5	April 20, 1941	Feb 28	March 15, 1945
Feb 6	Dec 17, 1936	Feb 29	Aug 3, 1944
Feb 7	Nov 17, 1949	March 1	April 14, 1940
Feb 8	March 21, 1946	March 2	April 14, 1949
Feb 9	Oct 11, 1940	March 3	July 24, 1947
Feb 10	March 16, 1937	March 4	Aug 19, 1945
Feb 11	Aug 19, 1945	March 5	Feb 16, 1947
Feb 12	Sept 30, 1942	March 6	July 7, 1943
Feb 13	Aug 18, 1942	March 7	July 29, 1943
Feb 14	May 21, 1942	March 8	June 9, 1948
Feb 15	June 12, 1937	March 9	Nov 11, 1943
Feb 16	May 10, 1945	March 10	Sept 6, 1948

Devotional Date	*He and I* Selection	Devotional Date	*He and I* Selection
March 11	July 19, 1939	April 3	March 20, 1937
March 12	July 29, 1943	April 4	March 27, 1947
March 13	Sept 19, 1940	April 5	June 19, 1942
March 14	Dec 19, 1940	April 6	Dec 11, 1947
March 15	April 30, 1948	April 7	July 24, 1947
March 16	April 28, 1949	April 8	Oct 17, 1940
March 17	April 27, 1950	April 9	Nov 19, 1939
March 18	Nov 4, 1948	April 10	April 26, 1946
March 19	Sept 12, 1945	April 11	Sept 12, 1940
March 20	Nov 6, 1940	April 12	May 16, 1946
March 21	Nov 11, 1948	April 13	Sept 30, 1942
March 22	June 25, 1937	April 14	Sept 6, 1948
March 23	Nov 27, 1947	April 15	Oct 18, 1945
March 24	Nov 4, 1948	April 16	April 21, 1949
March 25	May 2, 1938	April 17	June 1941
March 26	March 1, 1940	April 18	Dec 19, 1940
March 27	Dec 22, 1948	April 19	Feb 6, 1947
March 28	June 25, 1937	April 20	Dec 5, 1946
March 29	Aug 22, 1940	April 21	Feb 20, 1941
March 30	Nov 22, 1945	April 22	April 11, 1946
March 31	Oct 30, 1947	April 23	Dec 9, 1949
April 1	Jan 19, 1948	April 24	June 19, 1941
April 2	March 27, 1947	April 25	June 13, 1940

Devotional Date	*He and I* Selection	Devotional Date	*He and I* Selection
April 26	June 9, 1948	May 19	Feb 10, 1949
April 27	April 22, 1943	May 20	Feb 2, 1950
April 28	Sept 11, 1947	May 21	Dec 22, 1948
April 29	Sept 30, 1948	May 22	May 8, 1941
April 30	March 7, 1940	May 23	July 10, 1937
May 1	Feb 1, 1945	May 24	Feb 2, 1950
May 2	Dec 9, 1943	May 25	Jan 30, 1947
May 3	Sept 15, 1937	May 26	June 2, 1949
May 4	Nov 25, 1940	May 27	Jan 10, 1948
May 5	Oct 2, 1947	May 28	June 19, 1947
May 6	May 21, 1942	May 29	Oct 1, 1937
May 7	Sept 12, 1946	May 30	Oct 13, 1949
May 8	Dec 27, 1945	May 31	March 6, 1947
May 9	Jan 2, 1940	June 1	Nov 23, 1948
May 10	Feb 12, 1942	June 2	July 23, 1942
May 11	Aug 29, 1940	June 3	June 17, 1937
May 12	Nov 20, 1947	June 4	April 20, 1941
May 13	Dec 9, 1943	June 5	March 21, 1946
May 14	May 21, 1942	June 6	June 26, 1937
May 15	Sept 11, 1947	June 7	March 11, 1940
May 16	May 3, 1945	June 8	March 12, 1940
May 17	Oct 7, 1943	June 9	Oct 15, 1943
May 18	Jan 19, 1948	June 10	Dec 12, 1940

Devotional Date	*He and I* Selection	Devotional Date	*He and I* Selection
June 11	Dec 1944	July 4	April 28, 1949
June 12	Oct 7, 1943	July 5	Nov 28, 1945
June 13	April 19, 1940	July 6	Oct 2, 1947
June 14	Feb 3, 1949	July 7	April 1, 1938
June 15	Dec 19, 1946	July 8	March 18, 1948
June 16	May 30, 1946	July 9	July 1, 1937
June 17	March 15, 1945	July 10	Aug 26, 1943
June 18	Feb 10, 1949	July 11	July 25, 1946
June 19	Feb 20, 1947	July 12	July 23, 1942
June 20	Sept 12, 1940	July 13	June 20, 1940
June 21	Oct 24, 1936	July 14	Jan 17, 1940
June 22	June 3, 1948	July 15	Feb 26, 1948
June 23	Dec 16, 1942	July 16	May 20, 1948
June 24	Dec 24, 1939	July 17	March 1, 1945
June 25	Feb 6, 1941	July 18	Sept 26, 1946
June 26	July 1, 1948	July 19	May 3, 1947
June 27	Sept 21, 1940	July 20	June 30, 1937
June 28	July 25, 1946	July 21	March 28, 1946
June 29	Aug 8, 1940	July 22	Feb 13, 1943
June 30	May 30, 1946	July 23	July 4, 1940
July 1	July 29, 1948	July 24	Nov 25, 1943
July 2	Dec 30, 1948	July 25	Jan 20, 1949
July 3	Feb 11, 1943	July 26	Dec 24, 1940

Devotional Date	*He and I* Selection	Devotional Date	*He and I* Selection
July 27	July 11, 1946	Aug 19	July 5, 1946
July 28	Nov 25, 1948	Aug 20	May 20, 1943
July 29	Jan 3, 1948	Aug 21	June 25, 1942
July 30	Jan 3, 1948	Aug 22	Dec 8, 1949
July 31	Sept 12, 1940	Aug 23	May 11, 1940
Aug 1	Jan 29, 1948	Aug 24	Sept 1, 1944
Aug 2	Sept 6, 1948	Aug 25	Sept 12, 1940
Aug 3	Feb 17, 1944	Aug 26	Sept 10, 1942
Aug 4	June 12, 1938	Aug 27	Oct 27, 1949
Aug 5	Nov 13, 1947	Aug 28	June 28, 1945
Aug 6	Jan 10, 1946	Aug 29	May 21, 1942
Aug 7	Dec 28, 1936	Aug 30	Dec 8, 1940
Aug 8	Jan 4, 1945	Aug 31	April 17, 1938
Aug 9	Nov 10, 1949	Sept 1	March 6, 1947
Aug 10	June 2, 1949	Sept 2	May 31, 1937
Aug 11	May 23, 1937	Sept 3	April 16, 1942
Aug 12	Aug 6, 1948	Sept 4	July 10, 1942
Aug 13	Oct 4, 1938	Sept 5	July 2, 1945
Aug 14	June 25, 1942	Sept 6	May 4, 1940
Aug 15	Dec 13, 1944	Sept 7	March 29, 1940
Aug 16	March 11, 1940	Sept 8	Dec 22, 1949
Aug 17	May 21, 1942	Sept 9	July 2, 1942
Aug 18	Aug 29, 1940	Sept 10	May 19, 1949

Devotional Date	*He and I* Selection	Devotional Date	*He and I* Selection
Sept 11	Dec 1944	Oct 4	July 16, 1942
Sept 12	March 6, 1940	Oct 5	Dec 19, 1946
Sept 13	Oct 15, 1943	Oct 6	Dec 30, 1943
Sept 14	June 3, 1939	Oct 7	Oct 8, 1942
Sept 15	Dec 8, 1949	Oct 8	March 30, 1949
Sept 16	Dec 19, 1940	Oct 9	Dec 5, 1946
Sept 17	July 17, 1939	Oct 10	June 25, 1942
Sept 18	March 18, 1948	Oct 11	Dec 29, 1949
Sept 19	Dec 21, 1947	Oct 12	Oct 11, 1938
Sept 20	Oct 10, 1939	Oct 13	Oct 24, 1940
Sept 21	Feb 2, 1950	Oct 14	Dec 9, 1943
Sept 22	June 13, 1940	Oct 15	Aug 28, 1941
Sept 23	Feb 2, 1950	Oct 16	Jan 3, 1946
Sept 24	April 26, 1945	Oct 17	Sept 21, 1940
Sept 25	April 26, 1945	Oct 18	July 31, 1947
Sept 26	Nov 12, 1942	Oct 19	March 9, 1944
Sept 27	March 6, 1947	Oct 20	May 31, 1937
Sept 28	April 28, 1939	Oct 21	Sept 21, 1944
Sept 29	Feb 10, 1949	Oct 22	May 21, 1942
Sept 30	April 30, 1937	Oct 23	Sept 12, 1945
Oct 1	March 29, 1940	Oct 24	Feb 20, 1941
Oct 2	Oct 11, 1940	Oct 25	Oct 3, 1944
Oct 3	Oct 8, 1937	Oct 26	May 23, 1939

Devotional Date	*He and I* Selection	Devotional Date	*He and I* Selection
Oct 27	Jan 20, 1949	Nov 19	Sept 17, 1938
Oct 28	July 1, 1948	Nov 20	Feb 19, 1948
Oct 29	Aug 20, 1943	Nov 21	Dec 9, 1943
Oct 30	Dec 24, 1943	Nov 22	Feb 3, 1949
Oct 31	Aug 29, 1940	Nov 23	Dec 16, 1942
Nov 1	June 10, 1949	Nov 24	May 30, 1941
Nov 2	Dec 26, 1939	Nov 25	March 5, 1948
Nov 3	May 23, 1946	Nov 26	Oct 1, 1941
Nov 4	June 19, 1941	Nov 27	April 20, 1945
Nov 5	Jan 16, 1941	Nov 28	Jan 30, 1947
Nov 6	Nov 18, 1948	Nov 29	March 20, 1947
Nov 7	July 11, 1946	Nov 30	Oct 17, 1940
Nov 8	Feb 15, 1945	Dec 1	Nov 4, 1940
Nov 9	Oct 20, 1949	Dec 2	Jan 30, 1943
Nov 10	Dec 21, 1947	Dec 3	Dec 25, 1947
Nov 11	Jan 1, 1938	Dec 4	Dec 22, 1949
Nov 12	April 15, 1949	Dec 5	Jan 9, 1941
Nov 13	May 11, 1948	Dec 6	Oct 17, 1946
Nov 14	Feb 6, 1947	Dec 7	March 7, 1939
Nov 15	Jan 16, 1947	Dec 8	Dec 3, 1938
Nov 16	March 28, 1946	Dec 9	June 1, 1939
Nov 17	Dec 13, 1945	Dec 10	Feb 26, 1948
Nov 18	March 3, 1949	Dec 11	July 10, 1942

Devotional Date	*He and I* Selection	Devotional Date	*He and I* Selection
Dec 12	April 18, 1940	Dec 23	June 23, 1949
Dec 13	Aug 11, 1949	Dec 24	Jan 12, 1950
Dec 14	April 23, 1942	Dec 25	Dec 25, 1947
Dec 15	May 17, 1939	Dec 26	Dec 25, 1947
Dec 16	June 8, 1944	Dec 27	May 8, 1941
Dec 17	Feb 11, 1943	Dec 28	Dec 30, 1948
Dec 18	Nov 19, 1942	Dec 29	May 21, 1942
Dec 19	May 9, 1946	Dec 30	Oct 7, 1943
Dec 20	March 30, 1949	Dec 31	Sept 1941
Dec 21	Oct 2, 1947		
Dec 22	Dec 21, 1948		

Read the complete English text of the words of Jesus
as written down by Gabrielle Bossis.

ISBN 0-8198-3438-6
Paperback, 307 pages
$19.95

BOOKS & MEDIA

A mission of the Daughters of St. Paul

As apostles of Jesus Christ,
evangelizing today's world:

We are CALLED to holiness
by God's living Word and Eucharist.

We COMMUNICATE the Gospel message
through our lives and through all
available forms of media.

We SERVE the Church
by responding to the hopes and needs
of all people with the Word of God,
in the spirit of St. Paul.

For more information visit our Web site:
www.pauline.org

Pauline
BOOKS & MEDIA

The Daughters of St. Paul operate book and media centers at the following addresses. Visit, call, or write the one nearest you today, or find us at www.paulinestore.org.

CALIFORNIA
3908 Sepulveda Blvd, Culver City, CA 90230   310-397-8676
3250 Middlefield Road, Menlo Park, CA 94025   650-562-7060
FLORIDA
145 S.W. 107th Avenue, Miami, FL 33174   305-559-6715
HAWAII
1143 Bishop Street, Honolulu, HI 96813   808-521-2731
ILLINOIS
172 North Michigan Avenue, Chicago, IL 60601   312-346-4228
LOUISIANA
4403 Veterans Memorial Blvd, Metairie, LA 70006   504-887-7631
MASSACHUSETTS
885 Providence Hwy, Dedham, MA 02026   781-326-5385
MISSOURI
9804 Watson Road, St. Louis, MO 63126   314-965-3512
NEW YORK
64 West 38th Street, New York, NY 10018   212-754-1110
SOUTH CAROLINA
243 King Street, Charleston, SC 29401   843-577-0175
TEXAS
Currently no book center; for parish exhibits or outreach evangelization, contact: 210-569-0500, or SanAntonio@paulinemedia.com, or P.O. Box 761416, San Antonio, TX 78245
VIRGINIA
1025 King Street, Alexandria, VA 22314   703-549-3806
CANADA
3022 Dufferin Street, Toronto, ON M6B 3T5   416-781-9131